SHERLOCK
UNLOCKED

Also by Daniel Smith

How to Think Like Sherlock

The Ardlamont Mystery

SHERLOCK UNLOCKED

Little-known Facts About the World's Greatest Detective

DANIEL SMITH

Michael O'Mara Books Limited

In memory of my father-in-law,
Bob de Vekey (1940–2018)

First published in Great Britain in 2019 by
Michael O'Mara Books Limited
9 Lion Yard
Tremadoc Road
London SW4 7NQ

A CIP catalogue record for this book is available from the British Library.

Papers used by Michael O'Mara Books Limited are natural, recyclable products
made from wood grown in sustainable forests. The manufacturing processes
conform to the environmental regulations of the country of origin.

ISBN: 978-1-78929-069-1 in hardback print format
ISBN: 978-1-78929-092-9 in ebook format

1 2 3 4 5 6 7 8 9 10

Designed and typeset by K.DESIGN, Winscombe, Somerset
Illustrations by Aubrey Smith
Printed and bound by CPI Group (UK) Ltd, Croydon, CR0 4YY

www.mombooks.com

CONTENTS

INTRODUCTION

*There is nothing more deceptive
than an obvious fact*

SHERLOCK HOLMES, 'THE BOSCOMBE VALLEY MYSTERY'

What is Sherlock Holmes to you? Is he, as he is for millions, that figure in a deerstalker hat, smoking a curved pipe? Or perhaps in your mind's eye he is Basil Rathbone, or Jeremy Brett, or maybe Benedict Cumberbatch? When you think of Holmes, do you conjure up a master of deduction, an unfeeling brain without a heart? And what about Watson? Is he that buffoon so entertainingly depicted by Nigel Bruce, and rehashed by countless actors since?

Sherlock Holmes is so enduringly popular that he has become virtually detached from himself. Everyone thinks they know what sort of character he is, but our views are inevitably tinged by the effect of countless secondary interpretations of the original stories in which he appeared. That deerstalker and pipe were never there in Arthur Conan Doyle's tales of the detective. As you can read in the pages that follow, they were adornments added by an illustrator and an actor, respectively. That is what happens when a literary creation gains sufficient popularity to become a cultural property belonging to everybody. Holmes is in rarefied company in this respect – Dracula, Peter Pan, Harry Potter – creations that exist beyond the texts that birthed them come along only every now and again.

The idea of this book, then, is to go back to Conan Doyle's original stories of the world's greatest consulting detective and explore forgotten aspects of Sherlock Holmes – both the literary character and the cultural phenomenon. From clues in the text, we will explore everything from the personality traits of Holmes and Watson to the publishing history of the stories and the real-life cases that fuelled Conan Doyle's imagination. There will be tales of grisly murders, friendships between famous names, curious plot anomalies that got past both Conan Doyle and his editors, and much more besides.

Conan Doyle was one of history's great story-tellers. With an unstinting curiosity about the world, he crafted narratives that rip along and characters who – even when infuriatingly other-worldly, as Holmes can sometimes seem – are ultimately rooted in a profound humanity to which we can all relate. If Holmes were merely the 'brain without a heart' that he is sometimes depicted as, his readers would have lost interest decades ago.

But Conan Doyle had a complicated relationship with his literary son. While the world at large loved Holmes, his creator quickly grew weary of him. Were it not for the extraordinary financial incentives he had to carry on with the stories, Holmes might well have had a much shorter career. Indeed, Conan Doyle thought he had successfully killed him off after just two novellas and twenty-four short stories – only to find his creation was already starting a life beyond his control. This all meant that Conan Doyle did not always write the Holmes stories with the same eye to detail with which they have been read in the 125 years and more since. As a result, the tales are littered with inconsistencies and apparent errors that raise fascinating questions in their own right, all adding to the rich tapestry of the Holmesian universe.

A quick comment on terminology. The adjective 'Holmesian' – relating to all things related to Holmes and to those people who dedicate themselves to its study – is used widely in the pages that follow. I have opted for this terminology over the commonly used alternative, 'Sherlockian'. The words are, to a large extent, interchangeable, although historically Holmesian has been more widely used in Britain, with Sherlockian more popular in the US. As a born-and-bred Londoner who grew up in the southern reaches of the city, several areas of which make appearances in the stories, I defend my right to prefer the British variant!

You will also see many references to 'the canon' and things 'canonical'. The canon comprises simply the four Holmes novellas and fifty-six short stories (as published by the *Strand* magazine) written by Conan Doyle between

1887 and 1927. The founding texts, as it were. A great many were prefixed with the phrase 'The Adventure of. . .' when they originally appeared in the *Strand*, but for the sake of brevity I have rendered titles in their shortened forms in this volume. So, for instance, I refer to 'The Speckled Band' rather than 'The Adventure of the Speckled Band'.

There is no right or wrong way to enjoy Sherlock Holmes. If Rathbone or Cumberbatch *is* Holmes for you, that's just fine. Conan Doyle certainly wouldn't have worried. He, least of all people, believed in venerating his sage of Baker Street. But if the fancy takes you, this book will take you back to the author's original stories – a springboard from which you can dive into the fascinating wider world of the great detective as Conan Doyle envisaged him, full of forgotten facts and intriguing anecdotes. This is a chance, then, to unlock Sherlock. To paraphrase Holmes: 'Come, reader, come. The Game is afoot!'

What's in a Name?

Sherlock Holmes and Dr Watson are up with the likes of Romeo and Juliet or Catherine and Heathcliff among literature's most famous pairings. However, there was a time when Conan Doyle had other plans as to what his crime-fighting duo should be called. In early notes written in 1886 for the first Holmes story, *A Study in Scarlet*, he indicated the duo were going to be called Sherrinford Holmes (Sherrington Hope was another name under consideration) and Ormond Sacker (or possibly Secker – the handwriting is difficult to decipher). Thankfully, within a month or so, Sherrinford was cast aside for Sherlock and Ormond Sacker/Secker gave way to Dr Watson. Even the title of the book changed, from the working title *A Tangled Skein* to the version that we are so familiar with today. The question of the inspirations for the names of Sherlock Holmes and Dr Watson has long been a source of contention. Oliver Wendell Holmes Sr seems one of the more likely contenders for the detective's surname, given Doyle's self-professed admiration for the American physician and writer. Wendell Holmes was best known in Europe as one of the so-called New England Fireside Poets, who explored domestic and moralistic themes in largely conventional poetic styles. As for the origins of Sherlock, there are several candidates. There was a literary precursor in the form of William Sherlock who memorably appeared in Lord Macaulay's *A History of England*. Then there was a William Sherlock serving as a Chief Inspector in London, whose name regularly found its way into the newspapers of the time. But perhaps more likely is Patrick Sherlock, an old schoolmate of Conan Doyle from his days at Stonyhurst College. Alternatively, Eille Norwood – who famously played Holmes in a series of silent movies – said Conan Doyle once told him that he named his lead character after two cricketers. As for Dr Watson, it was long thought that his name was borrowed from James Watson, a medical friend of Conan Doyle when he was practising as a GP in Southsea on the English south coast. However, more recent analysis suggests that the two men did not meet until some time after Conan Doyle had already conjured up Dr Watson. So, a more likely candidate is Dr Patrick Heron Watson, an eminent figure in the medical faculty at Edinburgh University when Conan Doyle was a student there. Like his fictional counterpart, Heron Watson had become a military man after completing his medical studies, before eventually being medically discharged. Moreover, Heron Watson's obituary in the *British Medical Journal* in 1913 described a man of many notable achievements as well as an 'extraordinarily simple nature with intense affections'. It might have been a description of Holmes's own trusty comrade.

ORMOND SECKER

Incidentally, 'Ormond Sacker' was likely derived from London's geography – 'Ormond' coming from the famous Great Ormond Street Children's Hospital and Sacker/Secker from Secker Street in Waterloo, close to the Royal Waterloo Hospital. Meanwhile, Secker Street was near Stamford Street, which probably inspired the naming of Stamford, the character who initially introduces Holmes and Watson in *A Study in Scarlet*.

WHATEVER YOUR NAME IS!

There is an additional twist to the story of the genesis of Holmes and Watson's names. Given that they are only a duo, it would not seem unreasonable to expect some consistency across the stories as to their first names. Sure enough, Sherlock is only ever Sherlock. But Dr Watson appears both as John and James. To make matters worse, it is his first wife, whose maiden name was Mary Morstan, who throws the question of his nomenclature into doubt. We know from references across the canon that Watson's given name is John. So just who is this 'James' character that the fragrant Mary refers to? It is to be hoped that it is merely a slip of the tongue and not a reference to some rival for her affections. Moreover, we are told that his middle name begins with 'H'. The crime writer and great Holmesian Dorothy L. Sayer proposed a neat solution. She suggested that the 'H.' in Watson's name stands for

'Hamish', which itself is a derivation of James. So, Mary might be sharing an intimacy – a pet name based on a middle name unknown to the world at large. Certainly, Holmes displayed no reaction to Mary's use of the name, and it is hardly a thing that would have escaped his notice. The suggestion, then, is that she was in the habit of calling her husband James for innocent, if unclear, reasons.

Never Beeton

Sherlock Holmes's debut in *A Study in Scarlet* was published in *Beeton's Christmas Annual* in November 1887. Today, that magazine is widely regarded as the most valuable in the world. Not bad considering that copies sold for just a solitary shilling at the time. The first *Beeton's Christmas Annual* had appeared in 1860, the brainchild of the publisher Samuel Beeton, husband of Isabella, better known as Mrs Beeton and the author of *Mrs Beeton's Book of Household Management*. That title was first published in 1861 and sold millions of copies over many decades. However, by the time *A Study in Scarlet* was ready to be unleashed, both Mr and Mrs Beeton were long since dead and the annual that bore their family name was owned by the firm of Ward, Lock

& Co. Conan Doyle had hoped to receive a royalty dependent on sales for his story, but in a polite letter he was told that it was quite impossible as 'it might give rise to some confusion'. Instead, he was paid a flat £25 and in return surrendered the copyright in its entirety. The annual had sold out by the end of the month. Today, there are just thirty-four copies known to have survived, most of them in libraries. It is extremely rare for an edition to come onto the open market and, when they do, there is always someone willing to pay a premium. The record price was achieved at auction in 2007, with the winning bid coming in at $156,000. We can only imagine how much one of the two copies signed by Conan Doyle himself would fetch should they ever come up for sale.

The Opening Chapter

Four years before *A Study in Scarlet* first appeared, Conan Doyle set out to write his first novel. It was 1883 and he was working as a doctor in Portsmouth at the time. He was starting to supplement his income by short-story writing but was already frustrated by the tendency for such stories to appear without their author's name attached. Here was his chance to launch himself upon the world. With the not particularly promising title *The Narrative of John Smith*, it told the story of a fifty-year-old gout-sufferer compelled into a week of bed rest. Unsurprisingly, it was not big on dramatic plot swings: instead it was a connected set of discursive passages taking in everything from medicine to religion to interior design. According to its author, it had a 'personal-social-political complexion'. He sent off the text, which took up about four exercise books, to a potential editor only for it to go missing in the post, never to be recovered. Undaunted, he reproduced it from memory, although it never did find a publisher in his lifetime. However, in 2004 it was given a new lease of life when the second draft came up for auction and was bought by the British Library for £1 million. The Library published it in 2011, to the general delight of academics and enthusiasts, even though the tale pales against the Holmes stories. Conan Doyle himself may well have been turning in his grave. 'I must confess,' he wrote in his later years, 'that my shock at its disappearance would be as nothing to my horror if it were suddenly to appear again – in print.'

The Original Consulting Detective?

Sherlock Holmes himself suspected he was the world's first and only consulting detective, but a real-life counterpart may also have had a strong claim to that title. This potential rival was a gentleman of German extraction called Wendel Scherer. Around 1881, while touting his services as a private consulting detective, he found himself summoned to help investigate what became known as the St Luke's Mystery. It was certainly a strange case. A baker, who had himself come to England from Germany in 1870, was said to have returned one night to his home in Lever Street (in the St Luke's district of East London), never to be seen again. He had run a successful business but after his disappearance it was taken over by an old friend to whom he had given a part-time job. This friend, one Felix Stumm, was said to have grown close to his former boss's wife and suspicion soon enshrouded him. No body was ever recovered, making it impossible to make a murder charge stick, but Stumm was eventually sentenced to ten years' imprisonment for fraud. There are particular aspects of the case that suggest Conan Doyle may have been influenced by it when writing *A Study in Scarlet*. For one thing, the victim went by the name of Urban Napoleon Stanger, while the victim in Holmes's debut was Stangerson – hardly a common name. Then there is the significance of the German language in the story, not to mention the fact that Conan Doyle chose to locate his hero's home in

Baker Street, echoing the profession of the victim of the St Luke's Mystery. The evidence is not conclusive, but it is at least possible that Wendell Scherer was the prototype of the world's most famous consulting detective.

The Legendary Langham

When work finished on the Langham Hotel in 1865, it was for a while the grandest hotel in London. Located in the heart of Holmes's native Marylebone not far from Regent's Park, it was opened by the Prince of Wales (the future King Edward VII) and was the first building in England to be fitted with hydraulic lifts. The great and the good flocked there – among them the celebrated American man of letters, Mark Twain, and the French Emperor, Napoleon III. No wonder the hotel found its way into several of the Sherlock Holmes tales. It was here that the King of Bohemia stayed in 'A Scandal in Bohemia', as did the Hon. Philip Green in 'The Disappearance of Lady Frances Carfax'. Captain Morstan also enjoyed a sojourn there in *The Sign of the Four*. This was most apt because the Langham had played a vital part in the emergence of *The Sign of the Four*, the second story to feature the great detective. Conan Doyle was commissioned to write the novel during a dinner at the hotel – a get-together that has achieved legendary status in the literary world. On the evening of 30 August 1889, Conan Doyle arrived at the hotel to meet a magazine editor called J. M. Stoddart and a fellow writer – a certain Oscar Wilde. It was the first time Doyle and Wilde had encountered each other. Stoddart, meanwhile, was a man with an eye for talent and realized that here were two writers he would be happy to see in his publication, the Philadelphia-based *Lippincott's Monthly Magazine*. As a result of that dinner, Stoddart commissioned not only *The Sign of the Four* from Doyle but also *The Picture of Dorian Gray* from Wilde. Doyle's story (subtitled: 'The Problem of the Sholtos') appeared in February 1890, with Wilde's masterpiece following six months later. Not a bad return for a night's work by Stoddart. In his 1924 collection of memoirs, *Memories and*

Adventures, Doyle would refer to the Langham dinner as 'a golden evening for me'.

Get Me a Paget – Any Paget!

Many people – even Conan Doyle's own father (see page 47) – turned their hand to illustrating the Sherlock Holmes stories, but one stands out from all the others. No one played a greater role in shaping the popular image of Baker Street's finest than Sidney Paget, the man who illustrated Conan Doyle's stories for *The Strand Magazine*. It was not the pen of Conan Doyle that depicted Holmes in a deerstalker and Inverness cape, but that of Paget. (That look, for the record, was first sketched to accompany 'The Boscombe Valley Mystery', which appeared in *The Strand* in 1891.) However, had it not been for an apparent quirk of fate, Sherlock Holmes might have looked quite different. It is widely believed that Sidney Paget was commissioned to draw *The Strand's* illustrations by accident. The job was instead intended to go to his elder brother, Walter. So how did the mix-up happen? Sidney was one of nine siblings, and three of them studied art at the Royal Academy Schools. After graduating, he started to make a name for himself as an illustrator for various magazines in both the

UK and US, principally depicting war subjects in Egypt and the Sudan. However, Walter was the more famous artist by the time the first Sherlock Holmes short stories started to appear. He was particularly celebrated for his illustrations of Robert Louis Stevenson's *Treasure Island* and an edition of Daniel Defoe's *Robinson Crusoe*. According to legend, *The Strand* hoped he would take on the task of illustrating the Holmes stories and so sent a job offer through the post. It was addressed to 'Mr Paget, the Illustrator' or words to that effect, and – with several brothers all fitting that description – fell into the hands of Sidney, who duly accepted the commission. He would go on to produce 356 drawings to accompany 38 Holmes stories. To begin with, Conan Doyle was unconvinced by Paget's pictures, believing that he made Holmes more physically appealing than he had envisaged. Over time, though, he was won over. He even presented Paget with a wedding gift of a silver cigarette case, inscribed 'From Sherlock Holmes, 1893'. As *The Strand* would say of Paget, 'his delineations of the famous "Sherlock Holmes" stories had their share in the popularity of that wonderful detective'.

The Original Model?

Walter Paget may still have made a significant contribution to the public perception of Holmes. It is widely held that Sidney modelled his drawings of Holmes upon his older brother, a suggestion supported by Sidney's own daughter. Meanwhile, Alfred Morris Butler, an architecture student from Sidney's days at the Royal Academy, is thought to have served as the inspiration for his drawings of Dr Watson.

Becoming Sherlock Holmes

Sherlock Holmes is recognized by the *Guinness Book of Records* as the most filmed fictional human character in history. Rarely does a year go by without some new screen adaptation emerging. Not a bad achievement for a character once described by his own creator as 'not fitted for dramatic representation'. But, of course, Holmes predates the age of cinema and television, so it was on the stage that he was first dramatically recreated. The first man to star as the great detective was Charles Brookfield, who appeared in a short play called *Under the Clock* at the Royal Court Theatre in London. Conan Doyle was persuaded that Holmes might make a good subject for a play after all: he wrote a lengthy dramatic piece (some five acts in total) but was unable to find anyone of significant stature willing to back his project. He was, for example, rebuffed by two of the greatest actor-managers of the age, Sir Henry Irving and Sir Herbert Beerbohm Tree. His play instead found its way to an emerging Broadway producer, Charles Frohman, who sent it on to William Gillette, a celebrated American actor-producer-playwright. Holmes and Gillette created a kind of alchemy. Gillette freely played around with the script having received Conan Doyle's blessing:

'You may marry or murder him or do what you like with him.' Gillette's *Sherlock Holmes* opened at New York's Garrick Theatre on 6 November 1899 and was an instant hit, running for 235 performances. It then transferred to the Lyceum in London, where it ran for a further 216 shows and even spawned an immediate pastiche, *Sheerluck Jones (or Why D'Gillette Him Off?)*, at Terry's Theatre off The Strand. While Gillette's performance was not to every critic's taste, Conan Doyle heralded it as graced with the 'genius of a great sympathetic artist'. Gillette recorded the play in 1916 but all copies were thought lost until a copy was found in a Paris archive in 2014. After restoration, the movie received its second world debut the following year.

DEBUT OF A TRAMP

William Gillette ended up playing the title role in *Sherlock Holmes* over 1,300 times, becoming the first actor – but by no means the last – to become an international star thanks to his depiction of the sage of Baker Street. Another global icon, Charlie Chaplin, got his big break when he appeared in the play in London in 1901 as Billy the Pageboy.

A Baffling Performance

If Holmes's debut upon the stage was an almost unmitigated triumph, his first appearance on the silver screen was rather less confident. The first movie to feature the detective was a 30-second silent film entitled *Sherlock Holmes Baffled*. Made in 1900, it is considered to be the world's first detective film, although it can hardly be considered a satisfying watch on that score. The narrative (if that is not too bold a description) centres around Holmes discovering that his drawing room is being burgled. But as he confronts the thief, the villain disappears, only to reappear again – but not before Holmes has lit up a cigar. Holmes fires at the criminal with a pistol that he had in his dressing gown, but again the burglar vanishes. Holmes at least retrieves the swag bag containing his property – only for that to suddenly disappear and then reappear in the thief's hand. The thief then makes good his escape through a window, rendering Holmes utterly baffled. The film was made by Arthur Marvin, a cinematographer with several hundred credits to his name including some early productions directed by the legendary W. D. Griffiths. The names of the stars of *Sherlock Holmes Baffled* are, however, lost to history. A similar fate almost befell the film itself, before a paper print was found stored in the US Library of Congress in 1968. For a character who has become a staple of film and television, Holmes's screen debut gave little hint of the long career that lay ahead.

What Have You Done with Mrs Hudson?

Mrs Hudson appears in fourteen of the canonical Holmes stories, third only behind Watson and Holmes himself. The landlady of 221b Baker Street famously provided her tenants with regular sustenance, yet (in 'A Scandal in Bohemia'), Conan Doyle replaced her with a mystery woman going by the name of Mrs Turner. Despite Holmes being seemingly unfazed by her sudden appearance with a tray, we know nothing of her real identity. Had she briefly taken over from Mrs Hudson as landlady or was she perhaps an old friend covering Mrs Hudson's duties while she was otherwise occupied? We shall never know. Intriguingly, though, Mrs Turner almost made it into another story, having initially been inserted by Conan Doyle into the narrative of 'The Empty House', although it was Mrs Hudson who was restored for the final edit. In truth, Mrs Hudson is herself something of an enigma. Despite her many appearances, most are the briefest of cameos. We never find out her first name, nor do we receive a physical description of her. She has, we are told, a 'stately tread' but that is the only clue as to her demeanour. Holmes, meanwhile, considers her primarily in terms of her domestic talents – and he is not always particularly impressed. He describes her cuisine as 'a little limited' while admitting that 'she has as good an idea of breakfast as a Scotchwoman'. At least she fares well in comparison to the unnamed 'new cook' who appears in 'The Problem of Thor Bridge' proffering two underwhelming hard-boiled eggs, apparently as a result of the cook having been distracted while reading a romance in a popular magazine. Mrs Hudson in turn was remarkably tolerant of her frankly testing tenant. Indeed, according to Watson, he was 'the very worst tenant in London', being at once untidy, liable to play music at all hours of the night, prone to discharging firearms indoors and carrying out malodorous scientific experiments, not to mention being a magnet for violence and danger.

A True Gentleman?

But, in spite of Holmes's many flaws, dear Mrs Hudson was in awe of him and came to appreciate his 'remarkable gentleness and courtesy in his dealings with women' ('The Dying Detective'). Such was her warmth towards him that when he reappeared after his apparent death in 'The Empty House', she 'beamed upon us both as we entered'. Somehow, despite only a few enigmatic glimpses of her, we know instinctively that Mrs Hudson is a vital component of the Holmesian world. But as for this Mrs Turner . . . the jury remains out!

Lazy Parenting

Professor Moriarty was Holmes's arch nemesis – he was, after all, nothing less than the 'Napoleon of Crime'. Curiously, the canonical stories suggest that the Professor shared the same first name as his brother. Despite being the 'organizer of half that is evil and of nearly all that is undetected' in London, Moriarty only actually appeared in two stories, 'The Final Problem' and *The Valley of Fear*, and received mentions in just five others. In 'The Final Problem', his first name is not given but that of his brother – Colonel James Moriarty – is. However, in 'The Empty House', Holmes refers to his foe as 'Professor James Moriarty'. Two brothers, same name. The Professor was by common consent a mathematics genius, celebrated for his work on the academic paper *The Dynamics of an Asteroid*. In Holmes's estimation, he was also a masterful philosopher and abstract thinker. Picture then the tall, thin professor with his domed forehead, sunken grey eyes and a face that was 'forever slowly oscillating from side to side in a curiously reptilian fashion', pacing as he tried to fathom how this naming fiasco had come about. He could only have concluded that his parents' failure to give their sons a name of their own pointed to their singular lack of interest in their progeny. Even calling them One and Two would have suggested at least an attempt at differentiation. But to simply employ 'James' as a catch-all Christian name . . . So was Moriarty's extreme criminality a desperate bid for attention? Was this nefarious Napoleon simply trying to make the world take notice of him after his parents had failed to show much interest? It is a tempting hypothesis.

Wild at Heart

In *The Valley of Fear*, Holmes suggests a real-life counterpart for Professor Moriarty – the villainous Jonathan Wild. Wild lived an incredible double life in early-eighteenth-century London. With the city lacking an established official police force, he headed up a gang of 'thief-takers'. It was their job, in theory at least, to pursue criminals and bring them to justice, for which there would customarily be some kind of financial reward. They were, in other words, bounty-hunters. Wild, though, realized that he could become richer by running the thieves, too. It was reputed that almost every London thief of any note was under his command, stealing to order so that he could pick up a reward for the return of the stolen property. He also thought nothing of handing over to the authorities those thieves who were no longer of use to him, picking up further rewards in the process. One of the miscreants he captured was Jack Shepherd, a thief who had achieved folk hero status for his reputation for derring-do. Wild's part in Shepherd's downfall in 1724 saw public opinion decisively swing against the notorious thief-taker. Wild's wickedness now caught up with him and he himself suffered the hangman's noose a year later. The man who had claimed to be on the side of law and order, while secretly working to fatally undermine it, was derided by the public as the personification of corruptibility and hypocrisy. In Holmes's estimation: 'Everything comes in circles – even Professor Moriarty. Jonathan Wild was the hidden force of the London criminals, to whom he sold his brains and his organization on a fifteen per cent commission. The old wheel turns, and the same spoke comes up.'

For What It's Worth

While Wild is a contender for 'the original Moriarty', another possibility is a man nicknamed 'the Napoleon of the criminal world' long before Holmes conferred the title on his nemesis. Adam Worth was born in Germany in 1844 but relocated to the United States of America while still a child. His criminality soon escalated from petty theft to more serious robberies and, with the US authorities closing in on him, he fled to Europe. Setting himself up first in France and then England, he oversaw a criminal empire that practised robbery, fraud and illegal gaming – although he demanded minimal use of violence from his network of robbers.

The Gainsborough Affair

One of Worth's most infamous exploits was the theft in 1876 of a valuable portrait by Thomas Gainsborough of the Duchess of Devonshire from Agnew & Sons, a London gallery. William Agnew had paid 10,000 guineas for it just three weeks before – at the time, the record amount for a painting sold at auction. It is thought Worth stole it with a view to selling it on and using the funds to bail his brother out of custody. However, when his brother was released without bail, Worth held on to the picture to cash in at a later date.

It was Robert Anderson, an Assistant Commissioner at Scotland Yard most famously involved in the Jack the Ripper investigation, who first referred to Adam Worth as the criminal Napoleon, at least in part because of Worth's diminutive stature. In *The Valley of Fear*, Moriarty is described as owning a painting, *'La Jeune Fille à l'agneau'* by Jean-Baptiste Greuze (a picture that in real life was bought for a million francs in 1865). Some Holmes scholars suggest that this work was chosen by Conan Doyle because the *'agneau'* element of the title served as an oblique nod to the 'Agnew' theft, cementing the connection between Moriarty and Worth. Worth was at last chased down by the forces of law in Belgium in 1891 – his capture following a bodged robbery in Brussels – and he was sentenced to seven years' imprisonment. He was, however, released early for good behaviour and, in 1901, in a particularly audacious act, he sold the Gainsborough picture back to the gallery from which it had disappeared for a princely $25,000 – more than enough to bankroll a few months of the high life before his death in 1902.

Stranded

While *A Study in Scarlet* and *The Sign of the Four* were modest successes for *Beeton's Christmas Annual* and *Lippincott's Monthly Magazine*, respectively, it was at *The Strand Magazine* that the Holmes phenomenon really took off. Founded in 1890 by George Newnes, it was edited by Herbert Greenhough Smith from its first edition in January 1891 all the way up to 1930. The magazine was proudly mass-market and hoped to appeal across the ages, not least with its offer of a picture on every page and its half-shilling price tag (about half that of its chief rivals). Initial sales of 300,000 soon rose to half a million copies per month. Moreover, Greenhough Smith was a wily operator and a supreme talent spotter. He quickly recognized the potential of Conan Doyle's short stories, with the detective blooming in shorter-format narratives. *The Strand* published every one of the Holmes short stories, not to mention serializations of *The Hound of the Baskervilles* and *The Valley of Fear*. Conan Doyle also used it as a platform for several of his non-Holmes literary efforts – among them *Rodney Stone* and *The Exploits and Adventures of the Brigadier Gerard* – many of which were highly successful in their own right. But nothing came close to the popularity of Holmes, with his appearances customarily guaranteeing a hundred-thousand-plus spike in circulation.

LIGHTING THE TOUCH-PAPER?

Surprisingly, though, Sherlock Holmes did not feature in the first story Conan Doyle published in *The Strand Magazine*. *The Strand* was published monthly from January 1891 but Holmes made his debut only in the July. Back in March, Conan Doyle had contributed a story called 'The Voice of Science', which served as a gentle parody of provincial intellectual life. It tells the tale of one Mrs Esdaile of the Lindens, Birchespool, who serves as secretary for the local ladies' branch of the wonderfully named Eclectic Society. The narrative revolves around a gramophone – then a wonder of modern science (its appearance here prefiguring its later scene-stealing cameo in 'The Mazarin Stone'). Mrs Esdaile's intention is to wow attendees by playing a recorded lecture by a well-known academic. However, her son, Rupert, has other ideas as he bids to stop his sister, Rose, from being wooed by a certain Captain Beesly, who is to be in attendance. He executes a cunning ruse using the gramophone to ensure

Beesly's disgrace. Rose, meanwhile, ends up being courted by a far more suitable candidate. All in all, it is a perfectly amiable little trifle but gave barely a hint of the publishing pyrotechnics Conan Doyle was about to unleash through Holmes. In a relationship that ran from 1891 until 1930, *The Strand* printed 121 of Conan Doyle's short stories, 70 of his articles, 9 novels, 2 interviews and a single poem. What would the members of the Eclectic Society have made of it all?

TWELVE OF THE BEST

In 1927, just before the publication of *The Case-Book of Sherlock Holmes* (the final collection of Conan Doyle's Holmes stories), *The Strand Magazine* ran a competition. Readers were challenged to rank the twelve best short stories, with the winner being whoever most closely replicated Conan Doyle's own ranking. The generous prize was £100 and an autographed copy of Conan Doyle's *Memories and Adventures*. According to Conan Doyle, although he entered into the challenge light-heartedly, he soon realized that there was serious work to be done. He dismissed the dozen later stories included in *The Case-Book*, on the grounds that readers were less familiar with these tales. However, had he chosen to include them, he believed two of the *Case-Book* tales would have made it to his 'dozen best' – 'The Lion's Mane' for its plotting and 'The Illustrious Client' for its 'certain dramatic quality'. His criteria for inclusion were varied. Apart from originality of plots and a general sense of dramatic tension, he favoured those that, variously, introduced significant characters (notably Professor Moriarty and Colonel Moran), that had 'more female interest than is usual', and that displayed a 'historical touch'. Others he dismissed for faults that might have escaped the general reader. 'Silver Blaze', for instance, was dismissed because its 'racing detail' was 'faulty'. Nonetheless, he reassured his readers, he had striven to ensure all the stories were 'as good as I could make them'. Below is Conan Doyle's 'top of the pops' in full.

1. 'The Speckled Band'
2. 'The Red-Headed League'
3. 'The Dancing Men'
4. 'The Final Problem'
5. 'A Scandal in Bohemia'
6. 'The Empty House'
7. 'The Five Orange Pips'
8. 'The Second Stain'
9. 'The Devil's Food'
10. 'The Priory School'
11. 'The Musgrave Ritual'
12. 'The Reigate Squires'

THE IGNOBLE BACHELOR

Writing in the late 1920s in response to an accusation that the later Holmes stories were not as good as the earlier ones, Conan Doyle rated 'The Noble Bachelor' (published in 1892) as 'about bottom of the list'.

CRIMINAL PLOTS

Across the canon, Holmes takes on no less than thirty-seven cases of murder, attempted murder or manslaughter – homicide (most commonly by poison) being Conan Doyle's favoured crime for Holmes to investigate. Nonetheless, there are also fourteen cases of theft and robbery, four each of blackmail and kidnap (or false imprisonment), not to mention two tales that involve counterfeiting. Perhaps more surprising, some ten stories (over 15 per cent of the entire canon) involve no crime having been committed at all.

Sowing the Seed

Conan Doyle's first foray into the world of publishing had actually come way back in 1879 when, as a twenty-year-old, he had a short story in *Chambers's Journal* – a publication which aimed to be the journal of 'Popular Literature, Science, and Art'. The tale was called 'The Mystery of Sasassa Valley' and was published on 6 September that year. Subtitled 'A South African Story', it centres on the adventures of two young English fortune hunters in Cape Colony. Tom Donahue and Jack Turnbull are told by a neighbour, Dick Wharton, of the legend of the Sasassa Valley ghost – a hellish creature with glowing eyes. They venture to the valley where they catch sight of the apparently supernatural beast on a cliff. Marking the spot with sticks, they return in daylight to investigate further. They are overjoyed when they think they have discovered a large diamond but their hopes are soon dashed . . . but only for the time being. While firmly in the category of juvenilia, the story nonetheless hints at what was to come. There is an acute sense of adventure, an intriguing mystery, a hovering shadow of fear. It is fast-paced, if not as elegantly written as the classic tales of the older Conan Doyle. However, the author's name was not attached to it for many years. It was originally published anonymously and it was only in the 1890s that it was credited to Conan Doyle and then only in certain international editions.

The Price of Success

For most of his early life, Conan Doyle did not have much money, but he always harboured hopes that he would make a fortune from his literary skills. It was a risky strategy, but how it paid off! Back in 1883, he was a struggling doctor on the English south coast and his tax return for that year showed no liability – in other words, his income was insufficient to be taxed. When the tax man sent back his return with the comment 'most unsatisfactory' written across it, Conan Doyle returned it once more with a comment of his own: 'I entirely agree.' It was at about the same time that he sent his mother a letter in which he spoke of his determination to secure 'some three-figure cheques' for his writing. That would take a while, though. A Study in Scarlet brought him just £25 and The Sign of the Four about £100. By the time he signed with The Strand in 1891, he was getting

£35 per story for the first six Holmes stories (not bad considering the previous two works had been novels and these were but short stories) and then £50 for the next six – an indicator of how quickly Holmes's popularity had grown. He was, according to his correspondence, able to churn out four of the tales in a fortnight. But it was with the next dozen stories, commissioned in 1892, that he started to hit pay-dirt. For those twelve yarns he was paid a thousand pounds. After attempting to kill off Holmes in 1893, it was always going to take a big offer to entice Conan Doyle to bring his character back from the brink. Sure enough, in 1901 he received something near £5,000 for *The Hound of the Baskervilles*, then the following year he received an unprecedented $45,000 from *Collier's* magazine for just the US serialization of thirteen new adventures. While it is always problematic to attempt historical monetary conversions, it is safe to say that this would equate to a seven-figure sum today. Clearly, sometimes crime does pay.

The Sincerest Form of Flattery

Such was the immediate impact of Holmes's early appearances in *The Strand* that parodies of varying quality started to appear within months. More often than not they featured a detective whose name was a terrible pun based on the original, with the authors similarly adopting pseudonyms that were contortions of Conan Doyle's own name. So, for instance, 'The Adventures of Sherwood Hoakes' by A. Cone and Oil (pseudonym of Charles C. Rothwell) appeared in *The Ludgate Weekly* in April 1892. However, the original parody was probably a story called 'Robinson's Daughter', published a few weeks earlier in the comic magazine, *Ally Sloper's Half Holiday*. One of the most popular series of parodies appeared in 1893, when *Punch* magazine published 'The Adventures of Picklock Holes' by Cunnin Toil (pseudonym of R. C. Lehmann). The first wave of tales ran through to 1894, with another collection appearing ten years later and a final story ('His Final Arrow') coming out in 1918.

CHUBB-LOCK HOLMES

Another interesting addition to the parody genre was the 'Chubb-lock Holmes' comic strip that sprang to life in *Comic Cuts* in 1894. It was the product of no lesser talent than Jack Butler Yeats, brother of W. B. Yeats (winner of the Nobel Prize for Literature) and himself regarded as one of Ireland's finest painters of the twentieth century.

Where Angels Fear to Tread

Shortly after completing *A Study in Scarlet*, Conan Doyle decided to write a play that borrowed heavily from parts of that landmark story. *Angels of Darkness*, which he wrote around 1889, is something of a literary oddity, not least because it features Watson (or at least, a version of Watson) but no Holmes. The script essentially lifts sections of *A Study in Scarlet* and transports them to San Francisco. There are some fairly unpalatable scenes to the modern mind – particularly those that attempt to make comic mileage out of some crude racial caricatures. Watson, meanwhile, enjoys some undeniable sexual tension with a young lady called Lucy – a fact he almost certainly didn't go on to share with Mary Morstan (see page 69). Conan Doyle did not do much with the play once it was finished, presumably realizing that there were greater rewards to be had by writing more original Holmes stories instead. For a long while, myths about the contents of the script whirled around the Holmesian world, with the likes of John Dickson Carr believing it best that it never came to public light. It was nonetheless published at the turn of this century, intriguing as an item of Holmes apocrypha, but clearly a product of its time and with little to recommend a revival.

Carved into History

Being immortalized in statue form is an honour that befalls few literary creations. Yet Holmes can boast at least five major statues, spread across the world. The first to be unveiled, in September 1988, is to be found at Meiringen in Switzerland, not far from the Reichenbach Falls, which play such an important role in the Holmes legend. Sculpted by the English artist John Doubleday, it is the only seated statue of the great detective: for added interest it incorporates clues to all sixty canonical stories on its plinth. Just the following month, another statue was erected, this time at Oiwake in the Japanese resort town of Karuizawa. This location was selected on the basis that it was here that the translator Ken Nobuhara had added the finishing touches to the first full Japanese version of the canon. Yoshinori Satoh created the life-size sculpture. Edinburgh was the next to get its own Holmes, which appeared in Picardy Place (where Conan Doyle had been born) in 1991. This version – by Gerald Laing – is also life-size, depicting the detective with trademark deerstalker, pipe and cape. Then, perhaps belatedly, London took its turn. John Doubleday was again the sculptor and the project was funded by the Abbey National building society, whose main offices were thought to be on the site of 221b Baker Street. Again shown with pipe, deerstalker and cape, this one stands a mighty 3 metres high and is to be found on Marylebone Road, outside the entrance to

Baker Street underground station. It was unveiled in 1999. G. K. Chesterton had suggested a London statue to Holmes as long ago as 1927, so it was a long time coming. Then, in 2007, Moscow joined the party, unveiling a statue of both Holmes and Watson, located not far from the city's British embassy.

Art in the Blood

Based on an exchange between Holmes and Watson in the 1893 story, 'The Greek Interpreter', we know that Holmes was related to the Vernets, a famous real-life family of French painters. The conversation occurred one summer's evening as the two men discussed 'hereditary aptitudes'.

'In your case,' Watson told Holmes, '. . . it seems obvious that your faculty of observation and your peculiar facility for deduction are due to your own systematic training.'

'To some extent,' Holmes replies, 'but, nonetheless, my turn that way is in my veins, and may come with my grandmother, who was the sister of Vernet, the French artist.'

There were, in fact, three generations of Vernet painters so it is not entirely clear which one Holmes was referring to. However, it's safe to assume that Claude Joseph Vernet (1714–89) is too old to have been Holmes's great uncle (seeing as Holmes is thought to have been born around 1854). But his son Antoine Charles Horace (1758–1835), who was commonly known as Carle, could fit the bill, as might Carle's own son, Horace Vernet (1789–1863). Given the popular image of Holmes as both the epitome of Englishness and an icon of scientific rationalism, this particular aspect of his heritage is intriguing to say the least.

Drawn from Life

As Holmes claimed descendancy from the famous Vernets, so too could Conan Doyle point to an artistic strand within his family. Specifically, his father, Charles Altamont Doyle, was an accomplished painter and professional illustrator. He even got the chance to illustrate some of his son's work, although it is sad to reflect that his contributions are not particularly celebrated. It was a response symptomatic of a life dogged by problems and unfulfilled promise. Born in 1832 into a family of artists and illustrators (Arthur's uncle, Henry, founded the National Gallery of Ireland), Doyle illustrated a good number of books' including *The Pilgrim's Progress* and *Robinson Crusoe*, and was invited to exhibit his watercolours at the Scottish Royal Academy. Yet the success and adulation he craved remained elusive. Prone to depression, he increasingly took to drink and from the

1870s spent a number of spells in psychiatric institutions. Nonetheless, in 1888, he was given the job of illustrating *A Study in Scarlet*. If it was hoped that this might revive his spirits, the results were disappointing to say the least – the drawings reflecting a talent in serious decline. His health continued to spiral downwards and he died at an institution in Scotland in 1893. Arthur considered him a 'great unrecognized genius' whose life was blighted by his refusal to acknowledge 'the realities of life'. The author's enduring affection for his father is hinted at by the use of 'Altamont' as Holmes's alias in 'His Last Bow'.

The Name's Holmes . . . Sherlock Holmes

Arthur Conan Doyle originated a now world-famous phrase synonymous with another fictional hero of enduring appeal. Ian Fleming's James Bond is, of course, also known by the designation 007. The 'Double O' prefix indicates that he carries a licence from MI6 (Britain's foreign intelligence service) granting him the right to kill at his discretion in the interests of completing his field missions. Such is the powerful hold of the phrase 'licence to kill' that it provided the title of an episode of the film franchise in 1989. Yet Conan Doyle used those very words as a caption to a rather jaunty self-portrait way back in 1881. In August that year, he graduated from the University of Edinburgh with a bachelor's degree in medicine and a master's in surgery. In celebration, he drew an image of himself, behatted and wearing a suit, dancing while holding up his degree. Underneath is the legend: 'Licensed to kill.'

A LICENCE TO THRILL

While Holmes sometimes resorted to violence when necessary to solve a crime (and regularly armed himself with deadly weapons), he never directly killed anyone. No need for a licence to kill, then – just a licence to thrill, instead.

Dear Mr Holmes . . .

As Holmes's popularity grew, the less clear the boundary between fact and fiction became. This is exemplified by the extraordinary volume of correspondence sent to Holmes by people convinced that he was a real person who could come to their aid. From his early appearances in *The Strand* right through to the present day, he has received missives from a disparate array of correspondents. Nor have they come merely from over-eager fans or credulous child readers. The archives show that plenty of apparently sophisticated and well-connected adults, among them lawyers and police officers – have made contact in the hope of engaging his services. One of the first letters was from a tobacconist in Philadelphia seeking a copy of Holmes's monograph on identifying different types of ash. In another letter, dated 1913, a man named Felix de Halpert hoped to reach Conan Doyle at the 221b Baker Street address to ask for his assistance in investigating the murder of a Polish prince, which was likely the work of Russian agents. In the early days, letters sent to No. 221b were customarily redirected to Conan Doyle or Scotland Yard, although some also found their way to Joseph Bell and William Gillette, too. From the 1930s the Abbey National building society in Baker Street dealt with Holmes's post, employing a dedicated secretary to deal with the heavy workload. More recently, though, it has been the Sherlock Holmes Museum on Baker Street that has taken up the slack.

Disrespecting One's Elders

C. Auguste Dupin, the Parisian amateur detective created by Edgar Allan Poe, is often cited as the first great literary detective. Although he appeared in just three stories, 'The Murders in the Rue Morgue' (1841), 'The Mystery of Marie Rogêt' (1842) and 'The Purloined Letter' (1844), his influence on future generations of crime writers is incalculable. Like Holmes, he used extraordinary logical reasoning and close observation to unravel the most perplexing mysteries. Holmes, though, was rather snotty about his predecessor's capabilities. In *A Study in Scarlet*, for example, Watson commented that Holmes reminded him of Dupin, only for Holmes to respond: 'Now, in my opinion, Dupin was a very inferior fellow.' Holmes went on that he 'had some analytical genius, no doubt; but he was by no means such a phenomenon as Poe appeared to imagine'. Later, in 'The Cardboard Box', Dupin was this time damned with faint praise, described underwhelmingly as a 'close reasoner'. These critiques, however, were written with some irony by Conan Doyle, who never hid his admiration for Poe. He was, according to Conan Doyle, '. . . the supreme original short story writer of all time'. 'Each [of his detective stories] is a root from which a whole literature has developed . . . Where was the detective story until Poe breathed the breath of life into it?' In a 1902 preface to *The Adventures of Sherlock Holmes*, he went further still:

Edgar Allan Poe, who, in his carelessly prodigal fashion, threw out the seeds from which so many of our present forms of literature have sprung, was the father of the detective tale, and covered its limits so completely that I fail to see how his followers can find any fresh ground which they can confidently call their own. For the secret of the thinness and also of the intensity of the detective story is, that the writer is left with only one quality, that of intellectual acuteness, with which to endow his hero . . . On this narrow path the writer must walk, and he sees the footmarks of Poe always in front of him. He is happy if he ever finds the means of breaking away and striking out on some little side-track of his own.

An inferior fellow? *Mais non*!

Cock-Sure

Just as Dupin suffered under Holmes's scrutiny, so did another literary forebear – Monsieur Lecoq. 'Lecoq was a miserable bungler,' insisted Holmes. The Frenchman had, suggested the Baker Street detective,

> . . .only one thing to recommend him, and that was his energy. That book [*Monsieur Lecoq*, a novel published in 1868] made me positively ill. The question was how to identify an unknown prisoner. I could have done it in twenty-four hours. Lecoq took six months or so. It might be made a text-book for detectives to teach them what to avoid.

Monsieur Lecoq was the creation of Émile Gaboriau and, despite Holmes's protestations, the stories in which he featured (starting with a cameo debut in *L'Affaire Lerouge* in 1866) were a formative influence on Conan Doyle. In *L'Affaire Lerouge*, Lecoq was described as 'formerly an habitual criminal, now at one with the law, skilful at his job'. The character was based in no small part on Eugène François Vidocq, who had published his memoirs in 1828. Vidocq was quite the villain in his youth but was persuaded to become first a police informer and then an investigator. With first-hand knowledge of the criminal mind, he proved a smash hit at the job and eventually came to head the French national department of criminal investigations and established the world's first private detective agency. There were even rumours that he was the perpetrator of several crimes that he later 'solved' and his memoirs reveal a man who lived life as if it was a picaresque novel. Yet he also developed skills that Holmes himself fostered – from forensic analysis to mastery of disguise and thorough record-keeping. Lecoq was the bridge from Vidocq to Holmes, and Conan Doyle respected Gaboriau's achievement in bringing him to life. In particular, he admired his 'neat dovetailing of his plots', with *A Study in Scarlet* and *The Valley of Fear* in particular reflecting Gaboriau's preference for a structure in which the first half of a book focuses on the process of detection and the second half on explaining the circumstances that led to the crime.

Smoking Slippers

Holmes gave a whole new meaning to the term 'smoking slippers' by stashing his haul of tobacco in a Persian slipper in his rooms at No. 221b. This was just one of the many eccentric touches he brought to his legendary abode (which comprised two bedrooms and an airy sitting room bathed in natural light from two broad windows). Aside from great towers of books and papers and all the kit for his chemical experimentation, he also had a coal scuttle which he filled with further smoking paraphernalia, not to mention a bear-skin rug and a photo of 'the woman', Irene Adler. His post, meanwhile, was generally secured on the mantelpiece by means of a jack-knife blade. As for that Persian slipper, it might have been better used for its intended purpose, given the famous seventeen steps Holmes had to ascend and descend every time he came and went from his dwellings.

Mrs Hudson's Place

Descriptions of 221b Baker Street played an integral part in building up our understanding of Holmes's character, as well as serving as the jumping-off point for so many epic adventures. In fact, no less than forty-six of the canonical stories started here, with twenty-seven also reaching their conclusion back at Mrs Hudson's place.

Home from Holmes

But where exactly was No. 221b? At the time that Holmes and Watson lived there, no such address existed in the real world. Baker Street house numbers extended only up to 85. There is one school of thought that Conan Doyle envisaged his characters living on what was known as Upper Baker Street, at the northern end of modern Baker Street. Others, though, have interpreted hints in the stories (and particularly descriptions of locations in 'The Empty House') as pointing to a site significantly further to the south. The whole knotty issue was only made more confusing when London's urban planners decided to renumber Baker Street in the 1930s – a long time after Holmes's own residency had finished. The stretch of road that theoretically included 221 was now taken up by the headquarters of the Abbey National building society. Then, in the 1990s, the Sherlock Holmes Museum was opened on Baker Street on property stretching from 237 to 241 according to the modern numbering. Westminster City Council, however, took it upon themselves to recognize the museum's address as 221b – a designation challenged by the Abbey National until it departed the area in 2002. Quite what Baker Street's many postal workers must have made of it all over the years is anyone's guess!

A Place to Call Home

No. 221b Baker Street is among a handful of addresses that have resonance around the globe. It is, we all know, *the* home of the great detective. But it was not his first address in London. As is revealed in 'The Musgrave Ritual', that honour rests with Montague Street in the city's Bloomsbury area, from where he practised as a detective. His rooms there were described as 'just round the corner from the British Museum', a location with obvious appeal as Holmes liked to visit that venerable institution to gather information pertinent to his work. The Museum, based on the collections of Hans Sloane, dates back to 1753 and was opened to the public six years later. Its famous reading room – a magnificent circular, domed chamber set into the museum's courtyard – was designed by Sydney

Smirke and built in the 1850s. In Holmes's time, there was no more agreeable place to consult a book or an index in the whole of the country, and there was every chance he might bump into a public figure of the ilk of Rudyard Kipling, Bram Stoker or Oscar Wilde while perusing the reading room's myriad shelves. Montague Street ran (and still runs) along the eastern side of the museum. We see Holmes visiting the museum twice in the canon: once in *The Hound of the Baskervilles* to investigate the background of Stapleton, and once in 'Wisteria Lodge' when Watson learns from a casual aside that Holmes had made a trip there in the course of a fevered investigation.

The End?

After Conan Doyle died in 1930, it was understood by disappointed fans that 'Shoscombe Old Place', which appeared in *The Strand* in March 1927, was the final canonical story. Then, in 2015, there were reports of one of the great literary discoveries – a long-lost Holmes story written by Conan Doyle himself. A historian by the name of Walter Elliot unearthed the treasure in his attic – a charming curio of just 1,300 words, written around 1904 for inclusion in a 49-page volume called *The Book o' the*

Brig. The collection was put together to raise money for the restoration of a bridge that had been washed away in the Scottish town of Selkirk during floods in 1902. Entitled 'Sherlock Holmes: Discovering the Border Burghs and, by deduction, the Brig Bazaar', it is centred around an exchange between Holmes and Watson in which the detective displays his customary brilliance to deduce just how Watson intends to spend his weekend. It is no *Hound* or 'Speckled Band', but it is nonetheless engaging in its own way. Conan Doyle was very fond of Selkirk and, as well as contributing this story, he also appeared in person to open the fundraising bazaar. It is thought that the two-day event raised some £560 – a not insignificant sum at the time but one which pales against the value of the first Conan Doyle Holmes story to be discovered in nearly nine decades.

Off the Record

Although the traditional canon is taken to comprise *A Study in Scarlet*, *The Sign of the Four*, *The Hound of the Baskervilles*, *The Valley of Fear* and the fifty-six short stories that appeared in *The Strand*, Conan Doyle wrote several other short pieces that featured Holmes. The earliest was 'The Field Bazaar' from 1896, a short story written in response to a request from his *alma mater*, the University of Edinburgh, for a contribution to a charitable magazine. It was a rather post-modern affair, in which Watson and Holmes are seen having breakfast together, with Watson having received a request very similar to the one that had been sent to Conan Doyle in the first place. Holmes then sets about revealing the nature of the letter through a characteristic display of his powers of observation. Later, in 1924, Conan Doyle wrote the curiosity that is 'How Watson Learned the Trick' – a tale of just over 500 words specially written to be produced in a micro-format that could be included in the library of Queen Mary's Dolls' House, Edward Lutyen's astonishing giant-sized dolls' house created for the wife of King George V.

The Amateur Reasoner

In 1898, five years after killing off Holmes, Conan Doyle wrote two further mystery stories for *The Strand*, 'The Story of the Lost Special' and 'The Story of the Man with the Watches'. The first – about a train and its passengers disappearing – features a reference to 'an amateur reasoner of some celebrity', while the latter – about a dead man found on a train with several pocket watches in his jacket – also has an amateur sleuth at work. In both cases, the amateur makes impressive but flawed attempts to resolve the cases.

Numerous students of the Holmes stories have suggested that this was Conan Doyle's way of giving his hero an anonymous airing after several years of silence. Whether they add much to the core canon, however, is uncertain.

Smarter than Einstein?

No one can doubt that Holmes was smarter than the average, but just how intelligent was he? The detective himself was quite clear that some people are just born cleverer than others. 'It is a question of cubic capacity,' he once said. 'A man with so large a brain must have something in it.' So, in 1999, John Radford – Emeritus Professor of Psychology at the University of East London – decided to figure out just how bright Sherlock was. In his book *The Intelligence of Sherlock Holmes and Other Three-pipe Problems*, he scoured the original stories for clues and used three different methods of estimating the detective's IQ (intelligence quotient). He concluded, unsurprisingly, that Holmes displayed an extremely high level of intelligence – something in the range of 190. By comparison, Stephen Hawking and Albert Einstein are thought to have had IQ scores in the range of 160. While IQ may not be a perfect measure of intelligence (a fluid concept), it is nonetheless an important indicator of an individual's ability to think abstractly. Just imagine where we might be if, rather than fight crime, Holmes had used his talents to develop time travel or explain the origins of the universe!

Take It to the Bank

If we are to believe the words of Dr Watson at the start of 'The Adventure of Thor Bridge', the Charing Cross branch of Cox & Co. bank was home to a gold mine. For somewhere in its vaults was a 'travel-worn and battered dispatch-box with my name, John H. Watson, M.D., Late Indian Army, painted upon the lid'. It was crammed, so we are led to believe, with papers mostly concerned with Holmes's many investigations. If the canon gives us a taster of his peculiar genius, the Cox & Co. vaults offered the promise of a much larger feast. Cox's was undoubtedly a good choice for such a treasury. Founded in the mid-18th century, principally to facilitate the government's payment of members of the armed forces, it soon became the bank of choice for retired soldiers, such as Watson. Initially based in Whitehall, its head office moved to 16–18 Charing Cross, where Whitehall and Trafalgar Square meet, in 1888. In 1922, the bank bought the Henry S. King & Co. bank and rebranded as Cox & Kings, but was soon itself sold to Lloyds Bank and relocated to Pall Mall. Over the years, its role has changed so that now Cox & Kings is primarily a travel company. Yet despite all these changes, ardent fans continue to hope that Watson's trusty dispatch box remains buried in its bowels, to one day offer up its secrets to the world.

Arms and the Man

Both Holmes and Watson carried firearms in multiple canonical cases. Watson was still in possession of his service sidearm, which was probably an Adams revolver, while Holmes favoured Webley handguns. Holmes had good reason to feel the need to be armed. Across Conan Doyle's stories, he was attacked with, variously, a cane, a bludgeon, a knife, a heavy masonry slab, a horse-and-carriage, an air gun (twice), poison (three times) and firearms (four times).

A Good Reade

In *The Sign of the Four*, Holmes gives us an insight into one of the books that most influenced his own thinking – *The Martyrdom of Man* by Winwood Reade. He said of this text that it is among the 'most remarkable ever penned'.

William Winwood Reade, who lived from 1838 until 1875, was a British adventurer, historian and philosopher. *The Martyrdom of Man*, published in 1872, was intended as an over-arching history of Western civilization, divided into four broad sections: War, Religion, Liberty and Intellect. These abstract concepts are, Reade suggested, the historical drivers of human progress, with the 'age of the Intellect' set to bring an end to the period of war and religion. It is easy to see how such a thesis might have appealed to Holmes, the very epitome of intellect. Moreover, Reade suggested that while every individual may be a mystery, Man as a species could be understood in terms of scientific probability. Holmes gave this account:

> He remarks, that, while the individual man is an insoluble puzzle, in the aggregate he becomes a mathematical certainty. You can, for example, never foretell what any one man will do, but you can say with precision what an average number will be up to. Individuals vary, but percentages remain constant. So says the statistician.

Such a view clearly chimes with Holmes's own methods in seeking to understand the actions of the individual by a study of the mass. In 'Shoscombe Old Place', for example, he is heard to exclaim: 'Capital, Watson! A thumb-nail sketch. I seem to know the man.' It was by 'playing the percentages' – judging what the 'average' person might do – that Holmes ultimately was able to make one of his most famous assertions: 'Once you eliminate the impossible, whatever remains, no matter how improbable, must be the truth.'

Not So Elementary, My Dear Watson

It is the single phrase for which Sherlock Holmes is most famous. Yet he never actually said it – not in Conan Doyle's original stories, anyway. While he often said 'elementary' and 'my dear Watson', he never put the words together. The closest he came was in 'The Crooked Man' but even then the phrases were in the wrong order and separated by fifty-two words. The credit for coining the phrase in a literary context seems to lie with that genius of the comic novel, P. G. Wodehouse. It debuted in *Psmith, Journalist*, a story first serialized in 1909–10 and published as a novel six years later. At one point, Psmith is about to explicate certain events to his companions, telling them: 'I fancy that this is one of those moments when it is necessary for me to unlimber my Sherlock Holmes system.' When a certain Billy Windsor concurs with Psmith's conclusions, Psmith retorts: 'Elementary, my dear Watson, elementary.' Yet, there is evidence to suggest that the phrase had entered popular discourse even before Wodehouse's intervention. Way back in 1901, for example, an advert for Charles Ford's wondrously named Bile Beans for Biliousness presented itself as a Holmes pastiche and included the line: 'Elementary, my dear Potson.'

BIRTH OF A CATCHPHRASE

If it didn't come from Conan Doyle's pen, where had the line 'Elementary, my dear Watson' come from so that by the turn of the century advertisers were hijacking it for their own commercial ends? The great Holmesian scholar Mattias Boström has made a convincing case that it must have originated in William Gillette's celebrated play of Sherlock Holmes in 1899 (see page 26). While the line is absent from the original script, it seems likely that it found its way into the stage performance and from there into the hearts of its audience.

Not Even the Brightest in the Family

Sometimes it can be tough being a younger sibling. Such was the case for Sherlock, who found himself to be the intellectual inferior of his older brother, Mycroft. Some seven years senior, Mycroft lived in and worked out of Whitehall – that part of London that serves as the very heart of British government – and spent each evening at the Diogenes Club on Pall Mall, 'the queerest club in Britain' full of 'the most unsociable and unclubable men in town', each in search of an opportunity for silent contemplation. According to Holmes, Mycroft had 'the tidiest and most orderly brain, with the greatest capacity for storing facts, of any man living'. High praise from a man who Watson once famously observed was 'an isolated phenomenon, a brain without a heart . . . pre-eminent in intelligence'. According to Sherlock, Mycroft acted as a 'clearing house' of information and analysis for the government – a role to which he was well suited given 'his specialism is omniscience'. Where once he was considered 'a short-cut, a convenience', he grew to be 'an essential'. It is even said in 'The Bruce-Partington Plans' that he was 'the most indispensable man in the country' and 'occasionally. . . is the British government'. Mycroft was thus quite an act to follow but Sherlock did have certain advantages over his sibling. Specifically, he had a physical energy to which his corpulent brother could only aspire. Given the amount of racing around required in the field of criminal investigation, only the younger Holmes boy ever stood a chance of becoming the world's most celebrated detective.

Doctor, Heal Thyself!

. . . .

Doctor Watson had a traumatic time while serving as a doctor with the army. So disturbing were his experiences that he was not entirely clear whereabouts on his body he was hit by a near fatal shot on the battlefield. His military career began in 1878 after he qualified as a doctor at the University of London and signed up as an assistant surgeon with the Fifth Northumberland Fusiliers. Posted to India at the onset of the Second Afghan War, he was sent to Candahar but his experience was marred by 'misfortune and disaster' (the exact nature of which remained unspecified) and before long he was reassigned to the Berkshire regiment. On 27 July 1880, he found himself engulfed in the Battle of Maiwand. Facing an Afghan force headed by the famed military leader, Ayub Khan, the British forces suffered a defeat in which almost a thousand troops died and a further two hundred were wounded. Watson was among their number, receiving a shot from a Jezail (a typically hand-made, long-barrelled muzzle-loading weapon). In *A Study in Scarlet*, Watson clearly states that the bullet entered his shoulder, yet in *The Sign of the Four* the entry point had moved down to his leg. By the time of 'The Noble Bachelor', the reader's confusion is compounded by a reference to the Jezail bullet lodged in 'one of my limbs'. Fortunately, Watson's life was saved when a comrade by the name of Murray flung him over a packhorse that took him to safety. But while recuperating in Peshawar, Watson succumbed to enteric fever and returned to England with his health 'irretrievably ruined' and, presumably, his grasp of anatomy seriously compromised.

The Adventure of the Disappearing Dog

The question of Watson's wound is by no means the only mystery that surrounds Holmes's intrepid narrator. Another concerns the fate of a bull pup that Watson told Holmes he owned in *A Study in Scarlet*. This was, however, the only mention ever made of the poor dog. What happened to it? There is no suggestion that it ever found its way to 221b Baker Street. Mrs Hudson had quite enough to deal with in terms of her human tenants, so it is difficult to imagine she would have assented to the arrival of a dog as well. Some scholars have suggested that perhaps Watson was referring to this pet in symbolic terms. The dog, the theory goes, may have been emblematic of the low moods Watson suffered in the aftermath of his ill-fated military adventures and his return, penniless and somewhat lost, back in Britain. The use of canines to figuratively describe depression has a long heritage, after all – an example being the 'black dogs' that plagued Winston Churchill in his darkest moments. On the other hand, if we should take Watson's reference to the bull pup in literal terms, it is sad that the creature did not make it into other stories. It would doubtless have made a worthy companion to the pair, particularly given Holmes's penchant for using the talents of our four-legged friends in pursuit of wrong-doers (see page 141).

Serial Monogamist?

Yet another in a series of baffling Watson mysteries surrounds the number of wives that he had. We know for certain the name of only one spouse – Mary Morstan, who came into his life when she appeared as Holmes's client in *The Sign of the Four*. His attraction to her was clear from the outset, even as he hinted at a somewhat extensive history with the opposite sex. 'Her face had neither regularity of feature nor beauty of complexion,' he noted (somewhat unpromisingly, admittedly), before continuing, 'but her expression was sweet and amiable, and her large blue eyes were singularly spiritual and sympathetic. In an experience of women which extends over many nations and three separate continents, I have never looked upon a face which gave a clearer promise of a refined and sensitive nature.' The couple married a short while after the events of *The Sign of the Four* – in about 1889 – but by the time Sherlock Holmes returned from his Great Hiatus (in 1894), Mary had died. Holmes's reappearance, we are told, helped his erstwhile companion briefly forget his 'sad bereavement'. Yet by the time of 'The Blanched Soldier' (1903), Holmes talks of Watson having 'deserted him for a wife'. On the face of it, there can be no doubt that Watson has remarried, but to whom is never revealed. However, the subject remains a topic of hot debate among Holmesians. Some argue that Watson's 'bereavement' concerned the temporary break-down of

69

his marriage to Mary Morstan (a subject Watson would doubtless not have wished to share with his readers), and that they subsequently reunited. In other words, there was only ever one wife – Mary. The general consensus, though, is probably in favour of the two-wife solution. But other notable scholars have suggested anything up to six wives, based on hints and inconsistencies in the canonical texts, mixed with a good dose of conjecture. In 'The Five Orange Pips', for example, Watson originally referred to his wife visiting her mother. Yet we know that Mary Morstan's mother was dead, so some have assumed there was another wife who pre-dated Mary. In later editions of 'The Five Orange Pips', meanwhile, the reference to the wife's mother has been changed to the wife's aunt. Regardless, it is easy to see why Holmes once referred to the female sex as 'Watson's department'.

A Troublesome Son

If Conan Doyle initially enjoyed the runaway success – and the accompanying financial rewards – of the Holmes short stories he wrote for *The Strand*, it was not long before he grew to despise his creation. As early as 1891 he was confiding to his mother: 'I think of slaying Holmes . . . and winding him up for good and all.' His character was, he explained, a distraction from the serious historical novels he wanted to write, one 'who has tended to obscure my higher work'. This thought was still haunting him two years later when he wrote to his fellow writer, Robert Louis Stevenson, in response to Stevenson's slightly barbed compliments about the great detective. 'I hope you will allow me to offer you my compliments on your very ingenious and very interesting adventures of Sherlock Holmes,' he wrote. 'That is the class of literature that I like when I have the toothache. As a matter of fact, it was a pleurisy I was enjoying when I took the volume up; and it will interest you as a medical man to know that the cure was for the moment effectual.' Doyle retorted: 'I'm so glad Sherlock Holmes helped to pass an hour for you. He's a bastard between Joe Bell and Poe's Monsieur Dupin (much diluted). I trust that I may never write a word about him again. I had rather that you knew me by my *White Company*.' Sure enough, by the end of the year Conan Doyle had apparently thrown Holmes to his death over the Reichenbach Falls.

'KILLED HOLMES'

While hordes of readers were bereft after Holmes's demise, Conan Doyle was sanguine, noting in his diaries simply: 'Killed Holmes.' Of course, he was a rather less adept assassin than he perhaps realized and Holmes would come back to life, fuelled by the cheques that Conan Doyle couldn't bring himself to refuse. But Conan Doyle could never love his creation with the same passion displayed by his readers.

A Good Sport

....

The sport of rugby was a product of the nineteenth-century English public-school system, fuelling the snobbish idea of it being 'a thug's game played by gentlemen', as opposed to football which was a 'gentleman's game played by thugs'. Rugby plays a pivotal role in the 1904 story, 'The Missing Three-Quarter'. It is a gripping yarn concerning the disappearance of one of the key players for Cambridge University ahead of the fiercely contested Varsity Match against their rivals from Oxford. Although Holmes confessed to having no interest in the sport, he nonetheless praised amateur sport in general as 'the best and soundest thing in England'. A fact often overlooked is that Watson was, in his youth, an enthusiastic and talented player of the game. In 'The Sussex Vampire', it is noted that he used to play rugby union for the Blackheath team in London. As a man elsewhere described as 'middle-sized' and 'strongly built' with a 'square jaw' and 'thick neck', it is clear he had the physique for the game. Blackheath – in south-east London – was the world's first open rugby club (that is to say, open to anyone regardless of membership of a particular school or institution) and had the pick of the nation's finest players. In 1871, for example, when the world's first rugby international match was played between England and Scotland, the English side featured no less than four Blackheath players, including the captain. Given that Watson played his rugby for the club during the same decade, he was obviously no slouch.

Bowled Over

If Watson was a talent on the rugby pitch and Holmes was a force to be reckoned with in the boxing ring, their sporting achievements fell some way short of Conan Doyle's own. He was, for instance, an accomplished footballer who – playing under the name A. C. Smith – appeared as a goalkeeper for the amateur Portsmouth Association Football Club (a precursor of the modern-day Portsmouth F.C.). He also turned his hand to cricket, playing ten first-class matches for the Marylebone Cricket Club between 1900 and 1907 and being described by Wisden, the 'bible' of the cricketing world, as capable of hitting hard and bowling slow 'with a puzzling flight'. He scored a respectable 231 runs at an average of 19.25 per innings but took only one wicket. What a wicket, though! In 1900, he bowled out the greatest cricketer of the age, and perhaps even of all time, W. G. Grace. Conan Doyle would later celebrate the moment in verse:

> Once in my heyday of cricket,
> Oh, day I shall ever recall!
> I captured that glorious wicket,
> The greatest, the grandest of all.

If all that were not enough, he was also a decent crown green bowler, a skilful golfer and played a pivotal role in popularizing skiing among a sceptical British public. Conan

Doyle became a regular visitor to Switzerland in the early 1890s, prompted mostly by the hope of improving the health of his wife, Touie, who suffered from tuberculosis. It was suggested that the alpine air might prolong her life. It was at Davos that Conan Doyle discovered his love of the snow, taking on some hugely challenging routes. Writing of one expedition for *The Strand*, he said:

> But now we had a pleasure which boots can never give. For a third of a mile we shot along over gently dipping curves, skimming down into the valley without a motion of our feet. In that great untrodden waste, with snow-fields bounding our vision on every side and no marks of life save the tracks of chamois and of foxes, it was glorious to whizz along in this easy fashion.

Such invigorating prose played its part in persuading a generation of British adventurers to take up the pastime.

Heading for a Falls

As the man with the power of life and death over Holmes, it was in the summer of 1893 that Conan Doyle began to

devise the specifics of his murder plot against the detective. At the time, he was staying in Lucerne in Switzerland, where he was due to present a talk. While there, he found himself socializing with a group that included Henry Lunn (a church minister who would go on to establish a travel firm that became part of the famous Lunn Poly agency), Rev. W. J. Dawson (who edited a magazine to which Conan Doyle had previously contributed) and Silas Hocking (a novelist whose book, *Her Benny*, about the poor of Liverpool had been published in 1879 and sold in excess of a million copies). Conan Doyle declared to this circle that Holmes had become such a burden upon him that life was becoming unbearable. He was in search, he told them, of a suitable place to kill off his hero. According to Lunn, it was Dawson who first suggested that the Reichenbach Falls, near the town of Meiringen, might serve as a suitable spot. The suggestion struck a chord with Conan Doyle and in due course Dawson accompanied the author and Touie to the falls, where Conan Doyle could stare into the roaring cauldron into which he planned to launch Holmes. As such, Lunn would later describe himself as 'an accessory before the fact' in the purported death of Holmes, while Dawson called himself 'an unintentional accomplice'. But Hocking felt it was he who had been first to pinpoint the Alpine landscape as the ideal spot for a murder. 'If you are determined on making an end of Holmes,' he claimed to have said, 'why not bring him out to Switzerland and drop him down a crevasse. It would save on funeral expenses.'

A Whale of a Time

The 1904 story, 'Black Peter', centres on the investigation into the gruesome murder of an old whale- and seal-fishing captain by the name of Peter Carey. Carey, also known as Black Peter, died from being stabbed through the chest with a harpoon, pinning him to a wall 'like a beetle on a card'. In writing about Black Peter's previous ocean-bound exploits, Conan Doyle was able to draw on significant personal experience. In 1880, he had taken up

a commission with a whaling ship, SS *Hope*, serving as the ship's surgeon after a friend had been forced to relinquish the role. The vessel departed the port of Peterhead for the Artic on 28 February that year but was spectacularly unsuccessful in finding much in the way of whales. In six months, its crew killed just two. On the other hand, 3,600 seals were culled, along with five polar bears and two narwhals. Conan Doyle kept a vivid journal throughout the voyage. In it he related an incident where he fell into the icy water in his rush to join a seal cull. He was almost killed, first by drifting ice and then hypothermia. It was an event that earned him the nickname 'the Great North Diver' among his crewmates.

HARPOONED

On one occasion, Conan Doyle told the story of how one of those unlucky whales perished, lanced through the neck (perhaps providing the inspiration for Black Peter's harpooning). Despite his near-death experience, he was buoyed by the adventure of it all, reporting to his mother: 'I just feel as if I could go anywhere or do anything. I'm sure I could go anywhere and eat anything.'

Fiddling the System

In 'The Illustrious Client', Holmes likens his antagonist in the story, Baron Gruner, to one of the most colourful real-life criminals of the nineteenth century, Charles Peace. 'A complex mind,' Holmes said. 'All great criminals have that. My old friend Charlie Peace was a violin virtuoso. Wainwright was no mean artist. I could quote many more.' But just who was Charles Peace? Born in 1832, he spent long stretches of his life travelling between towns and cities, trading bric-a-brac and consolidating his income by playing the violin to a very high standard. He was also a career-burglar and in 1876 became a murderer, too. First, he killed a police officer, Nicholas Cock, who had tried to apprehend him in Manchester during an attempted break-in. Then, later the same year, in Sheffield, he shot dead his neighbour, Arthur Dyson, whose wife he had taken a fancy to. He then went on the run, fleeing to London, but was arrested during another attempted burglary in the well-to-do suburb of Blackheath in 1878. Charged with the Dyson murder, he went on trial in Leeds and was executed early the following year. The Wainwright to whom Holmes referred, meanwhile, was Thomas Griffiths Wainewright (Conan Doyle missed out the 'e' in his surname). Born into affluence in 1794, he was orphaned at a young age and, though a talented artist (he exhibited at the Royal Academy), was beset by financial problems. A forger, he was found guilty of fraud against the Bank of England in

1837 and was transported to the Australian penal colony of Van Diemen's Land (modern-day Tasmania). He was also suspected of killing at least three people for financial gain, although he never answered any such charges. He lived out a further decade in Van Diemen's Land, during which he produced portraits of the colony's social elite.

The Guy's in Disguise

Holmes once admitted that the 'touch of the artist wells up within me, and calls insistently for a well-staged performance', while Watson described him as 'the master dramatist'. This sense of theatricality was reflected in his penchant for donning a disguise, something he did with admirable skill. In the canonical stories he variously posed as sailors and sea captains, general workmen, men of the cloth, a boozy groom, a plumber, an elderly lady, an Irish-American agent, a Norwegian explorer, an opium addict, a bookseller, an 'old sporting man' and a layabout.

Ringing a Bell

When *The Adventures of Sherlock Holmes*, the first short-story collection, was published in 1892, it was dedicated 'To My Old Teacher, Joseph Bell'. Bell, Conan Doyle made clear, had been the true-life inspiration for his literary detective. He had been one of Conan Doyle's teachers when he had studied medicine at Edinburgh University in the 1870s, and had even employed him as his medical assistant. Bell was famous among his students for an unnerving ability to pick up on the smallest non-verbal clues to establish a subject's background. He could, for instance, discover where someone lived from traces of soil on their shoes, or establish their occupations from their gait or the way they sported a hat. Conan Doyle studied Bell's methods and extended them into the character of Holmes. In 1892, he wrote to Bell: 'It is most certainly to you that I owe Sherlock Holmes . . . Round the centre of deduction and inference and observation which I heard you inculcate,' he said, 'I have tried to build up a man who pushed the thing as far as it would go . . .' Holmes elucidated Bell's method in *A Study in Scarlet*:

> By a man's fingernails, by his coat-sleeve, by his boot, by his trouser knees, by the callosities of his forefinger and thumb, by his expression, by his shirt cuffs – by each of these things a man's calling is plainly revealed. That all united should fail to enlighten the competent enquirer in any case is almost inconceivable.

What was less well known at the time was that Bell had spent the previous twenty years investigating a string of perplexing criminal cases with Dr Henry Littlejohn, another member of the Edinburgh University medical faculty. Littlejohn was Edinburgh's police surgeon, which meant he was the first medical man on the scene of countless crimes in Scotland throughout the second half of the twentieth century. He was also a pioneer in the then nascent discipline of forensics – the use of scientific methodology in the practice of criminal investigation. It was almost certainly him that first introduced Conan Doyle to many cutting-edge forensic techniques (including crime scene analysis) that he weaved so deftly into the Holmes stories. Yet it was only in 1929, long after Littlejohn's death, that Conan Doyle acknowledged Littlejohn's influence. Bell and Littlejohn, he said, had inspired him to write detective stories from 'the point of view of the scientific man'.

Losing the Plot

As well as serving as a model for Sherlock Holmes, it is known that Joseph Bell also offered some story ideas to Conan Doyle. Indeed, in the early days of Holmes, the author is said to have asked his mentor to set aside ten minutes or so a day to think up story ideas since he was 'insatiable for material'. A letter from Conan Doyle to Bell in 1892 thanked him 'very heartily' for the 'tips' and alluded to a Bell-inspired plot (apparently never actually used): 'The deserter-cobbler is admirable. I wish I had a dozen more such cases.' It was around this time that Bell also suggested that Holmes go up against a killer who used a bacterial agent as his weapon. Bell suggested he had knowledge of just such a case. Conan Doyle, though, was not sure, fearing that such a plot might be too much for his readership. In the 1920s, Conan Doyle would write that he had generally found Bell's plot suggestions to be impractical for his needs. Yet, there is something strangely familiar about that germ-murderer idea. In 1913, Holmes appeared in 'The Dying Detective' – a tale that pivots around a dastardly killer's attempts to take his victims by infecting them with a little-known disease originating in Asia. Whether or not Conan Doyle had forgotten Bell's suggestion of a bio-murderer all those years ago, we will never know. But surely the old doctor had sown a seed that blossomed into one of the great canonical tales, which was published shortly after his own death.

School of Scandal

Opium regularly crops up in the canonical stories, most often in the context of willing experimentation. There are also a couple of instances of opium poisoning, notably in 'Silver Blaze' and 'Wisteria Lodge'. Intriguingly, Conan Doyle had an early-life run-in of his own with one of the most notorious opium poisoners in Scottish history. In the autumn of 1866, the future author began studies at Edinburgh's Newington Academy, located just a few streets from his home. Shortly before his arrival, a Frenchman by the name of Eugene Chantrelle had been employed to teach modern languages. It was not long, though, before Chantrelle was forced out, having begun an affair with a fifth-former, Elizabeth Cullen Dyer, who fell pregnant. The teacher and the girl subsequently married but on 2 January 1878, Elizabeth died at her home, seemingly the victim of accidental gas poisoning. However, further investigations (most notably by Holmes's mentor, Joseph Bell, and his colleague, Henry Littlejohn) revealed that her death was in fact the result of deliberate opium poisoning. Chantrelle was duly found guilty of murdering his wife, and sentenced to hang.

A NICE COMPLIMENT

As Chantrelle stood on the gallows, he turned to Henry Littlejohn (who was attending in an official capacity), doffed his hat and said: 'Bye-bye, Littlejohn. Don't forget to give my compliments to Joe Bell. You both did a good job in bringing me to the scaffold.' The murder and trial caused a sensation that Conan Doyle no doubt followed in the newspapers. As Conan Doyle created his own characters who wielded opium with malicious intent, the spectre of Chantrelle, his old teacher, must surely have been hanging over him.

Defending the Family Honour

Although Conan Doyle was himself generous in his recognition of Joseph Bell, others of his family would prove more reluctant to acknowledge his mentor's contribution – in particular, his son Adrian Conan Doyle. Conan Doyle Snr had five children altogether, two with his first wife, Touie, and three with his second wife, Jean. Adrian was his youngest son, born in 1910 to Jean. He proved to be a robust defender of his father's legacy and took notable exception to a biography of Arthur written by Hesketh Pearson in 1943. He responded by publishing his own take on his father, firstly in extended essay form ('Conan Doyle: His Life and Art', 1943) and then, two years later, in the full-length *The True Conan Doyle*. One of the thrusts of Adrian's text was that his father had been the 'real' Sherlock Holmes, not Bell or any other pretenders to the throne. Referring specifically to Bell, he spoke of 'the ridiculous position that could arise if the plaudits due to a brilliant virtuoso were reserved only for the teacher who gave him his original music lessons'.

I, HOLMES

'Mr Hayden Coffin, the American journalist,' Adrian once wrote, 'has offered us interesting confirmation . . . that my father told him in a private interview in 1918 that – "If anyone is Holmes, then I must confess that it is I."' He also cited Arthur's own words in evidence: '. . . a man cannot spin a character out of his own inner consciousness and make it really lifelike unless he has some possibilities of that character within him.'

According to Adrian: 'In power of deductive observation I have never known his equal.' He even described how his father had owned a 'dust-red dressing gown' and a curved pipe – items, he rather tenuously suggested, with which in 'the mind's eye, we surely visualize the Master'. His opinion echoed the sentiments of his mother, who in 1934 had written: 'The public does not realize that my husband had the Sherlock Holmes brain, and that sometimes he privately solved mysteries that had non-plussed the police.' It is possible to understand Adrian's frustration that, as he saw it, his father was being stripped of some of the credit for the character of Sherlock Holmes when, of course, he was the product first and foremost of Conan Doyle's mind. However, it is possible that there were other factors at play in Adrian's vehement downplaying of Bell's role in the detective's genesis. Bell had, after all, been asked by Conan Doyle to assist with possible plotlines and certainly contributed several ideas. Did Adrian – a man who kept an eye on the bottom line – fear that if Bell was too widely acknowledged, one or more of his descendants might come looking for some financial recompense? It would perhaps explain why Adrian seemed so much more bothered than his own father that Bell had been bathed in Holmes's reflected glory.

The Islander Who Wasn't

* *

The Sign of the Four features a native of the Andaman Islands by the name of Tonga. However, there is little chance that Tonga hailed from the Andamans, which lie in the Bay of Bengal. Instead, he is a reflection of the popular perception of 'exotic savages' that prevailed in Victorian Britain – an idea rooted in imperialist aspirations rather than anthropological fact. Holmes sought background on the poisoned dart-blowing Tonga from a recently published gazetteer. The aborigines of the Andaman Islands, it said,

> . . .may perhaps claim the distinction of being the smallest race upon this earth, though some anthropologists prefer the Bushmen of Africa, the Digger Indians of America, and the Terra del Fuegians. The average height is rather below four feet, although many full-grown adults may be found who are very much smaller than this. They are a fierce, morose, and intractable people, though capable of forming most devoted friendships when their confidence has once been gained. They are naturally hideous, having large, misshapen heads, small, fierce eyes, and distorted features. Their feet and hands, however, are remarkably small.

It just so happens that even to this day, the native groups of the Andamans have had remarkably little interaction with the outside world. At the time Conan Doyle was writing, very little was understood about the islands except that attempts to establish a British colony in the late eighteenth century were quickly abandoned. Fresh in the memory, too, was the murder in 1872 of the British Viceroy by a convict of the penal colony established by the British there in the 1850s. The anthropological information that Holmes read, however, does not correspond to the known characteristics of any of its indigenous groups. In other words, Tonga was almost certainly not the Andamans native that Holmes believed him to be.

When Doctors Go Wrong

Watson is the very essence of the reliable, adept and good-hearted medical man, but not all of the doctors who appear in the canonical stories come across quite so well. It was in 'The Speckled Band' that Holmes made the observation: 'When a doctor does go wrong he is the first of criminals. He has nerve and he has knowledge. Palmer and Pritchard were among the heads of their profession.' Here, Conan Doyle once again wove details from real life into Holmes's fictional world. The doctors cited, William Palmer and

Edward Pritchard, were reviled murderers of relatively recent vintage. Both were, in truth, ostensibly reliable local GPs rather than the 'heads of their profession' as Holmes suggested, unless the profession he was referring to was the killing one. Certainly, neither paid much heed to the demands of their Hippocratic Oath. Palmer was convicted of murdering a friend, John Cook, in 1855 by means of strychnine, apparently so that he could claim the victim's substantial gambling winnings for himself. Palmer was also suspected of murdering, among others, his own brother, mother-in-law and even four of his children (each of whom succumbed to 'convulsions' before their first birthdays). In each case, the alleged motive was financial. No lesser figure than Charles Dickens called Palmer 'the greatest villain that ever stood in the Old Bailey'. He was hanged in 1856. Pritchard, meanwhile, was also accused of being a poisoner, with his wife and mother-in-law among his victims. It is likely he also killed a servant girl, with the existence of an uncomfortable *ménage-à-trois* in the Glasgow family home put forward as motive. He was convicted and hanged in 1856. Pritchard had a couple of intriguing links to Conan Doyle, too. The first was that he hailed from Southsea, in Hampshire, where Conan Doyle for a time practised as a doctor. Secondly, Henry Littlejohn (see page 80) helped gather together the forensic evidence for the Crown's case against the miscreant doctor.

Something to Steady the Nerves

A prolific smoker and not insignificant drug-taker, Holmes at least took his alcohol in moderation. He was a red-wine drinker, favouring claret (imbibed in at least two stories) and also Beaune (a burgundy), which he drank at lunch with Watson in *The Sign of the Four*. As for spirits, he was most likely to go for whisky. As would be expected given Conan Doyle's roots, it is most certainly Scotch whisky that he would have drunk. He is seen drinking it twice in the

canonical stories, each time mixed with soda, and offering it to others a further three times (once in combination with soda and twice with water). However, when Holmes and Watson wanted to fortify others with a drop of alcohol, they most commonly turned to brandy, which they wielded on no less than five occasions in the original stories.

Déjà Vu

At the beginning of 'The Cardboard Box', Holmes puts on a bravura performance in which he seems to have been able to read the mind of Watson. (He hasn't, of course, but has merely picked up on a series of subtle clues.) Yet there is something else remarkable about this episode – it appears, word for word, in 'The Resident Patient', too. The explanation involves a strange quirk of publishing history. 'The Cardboard Box' has some of the most gruesome imagery in all the canon – that of severed ears. Possibly because of its shocking nature, the story was not published in the original British edition of *The Memoirs of Sherlock Holmes*, although it did appear briefly in the American version before being removed. With the story effectively out of circulation, Conan Doyle lifted the relevant passage (of which he was clearly proud) and inserted it into a new story. However, with the passage of time 'The Cardboard Box' found its way into British versions of *The Memoirs* (and in America, the volume entitled *His Last Bow*). So today, eagle-eyed readers can enjoy the extract not once but twice in any volume of the complete canonical works – although those ears still have the power to shock!

Bar Flies

The Criterion Bar and Restaurant in London's Piccadilly Circus, is so proud of its Holmesian associations that in 1953 a commemorative blue plaque was unveiled to celebrate a meeting that never really happened within its walls. For it is here, so we are told in *A Study in Scarlet*, that Watson is standing at the bar when he receives a tap on the shoulder. Watson turns to see Stamford, his old dresser (in other words, his medical assistant) from his days studying at St Bart's. It is, of course, Stamford who alerts Watson to the possibility of sharing rooms with an acquaintance who was 'bemoaning himself this morning because he could not get someone to go halves with him in some nice rooms which he had found, and which were too much for his purse'. Although Stamford warns that Watson might 'not care for him as a constant companion', Watson is not to be deterred and so begins one of the most enduring literary relationships of all time. The Criterion itself had only opened in 1873, a spectacular meeting-spot done out in the Neo-Byzantine style. It soon garnered a devoted clientele, which included such literary luminaries as H. G. Wells.

The Game is Afoot!

'Come, Watson, come!' Holmes once famously cried. 'The game is afoot.' He borrowed the latter expression from Shakespeare (*Henry IV, Part 1*) and 'the Game' has come to be a vital part of the Holmesian experience. Among Holmesians, 'the Game' refers to efforts to resolve queries and inconsistencies and to fill in gaps that spring from Conan Doyle's original body of stories by picking up on small details and expounding new theories. Practitioners tend to throw themselves wholeheartedly into the pastime even as they recognize its essential frivolity. But, just as the player of the Game might seek to establish the origins of Holmes and Watson, we might ask what the origins of the Game are itself. Its inventor is generally acknowledged to be Ronald Knox, an English priest and sometime-crime-novelist. In 1911, he authored an article entitled 'Studies in the Literature of Sherlock Holmes', which he delivered to the Gryphon Club at Trinity College, Oxford. 'If there is anything pleasant in life, it is doing what we aren't meant to do,' he began.

> . . . It is the method by which we treat as significant what the author did not mean to be significant, by which we single out as essential what the author regarded as incidental. There is, however, a special fascination in applying this method to Sherlock Holmes, because it is, in a sense, Holmes's own method. 'It has long been

an axiom of mine,' he says, 'that the little things are infinitely the most important.' It might be the motto of his life's work. And it is, is it not, as we clergymen say, by the little things, the apparently unimportant things, that we judge of a man's character.

So began a new school of Holmesian study based around the Game.

The Real Expert

Conan Doyle himself was once moved to comment to Knox: 'I cannot help writing to you to tell you of the amusement – and also the amazement – with which I read your article on Sherlock Holmes. That anyone should spend such pains on such material was what surprised me. Certainly you know a great deal more about it than I do . . .'

The Right Tools

Watson once declared that he had become an institution in the life of Holmes, much like his violin. But what a violin! On the face of it, Sherlock Holmes was in possession of an instrument manufactured by the most famous name in the business – Stradivarius. He had bought it on London's Tottenham Court Road for a mere 55 shillings, though it was said to be valued at something more than 500 guineas. Given how rarely the wool was pulled over Holmes's eyes, we must assume his purchase of the violin really was one of the greatest deals of his life. It was, after all, a source of great solace for the detective, helping him work through complicated cases and serving as a means of winding down once an investigation was completed. In his darker moments, he seemed to gain some comfort from just simply clutching it. He was a talented, if slightly erratic, player, Watson calling his skills 'remarkable, but as eccentric as all his other accomplishments'. Sometimes, he would indulge Watson by playing a whole series of the doctor's favourite airs. Holmes was also known to be a fan of the work of Felix Mendelssohn, Frédéric Chopin, Richard Wagner and Jacques Offenbach. Of the celebrated player Niccolò Paganini, meanwhile, he would regale Watson with 'anecdote after anecdote of this extraordinary man'. In rather more weary terms, Watson also described him 'prattling' about the differences between Stradivarii and Cremona violins.

MINDS IN CONCERT

Holmes's love of the violin was such that it underpinned a large part of his relatively limited social life. In *A Study in Scarlet*, for example, he made a special effort to see a performance by Wilhelmine Norman-Neruda. Born into a family with rich musical heritage in Brno (at the time part of the Austrian Empire), Norman-Neruda confounded critics who did not believe the violin was a suitable instrument for a woman. Performing in public from the age of seven, she went on to marry the Swedish musician Ludvig Norman and then the Anglo-German Charles Hallé (founder of the Hallé Orchestra). She was appointed Violinist to the Queen in 1901 and Holmes commended her 'attack and her bowing' as 'splendid'. In 'The Red-Headed League', Holmes also took time to attend a concert by the violinist and composer, Martín Melitón Pablo de Sarasate y Navascués, at St James's Hall. Holmes was in good company in his appreciation of Sarasate. George Bernard Shaw was another fan, describing his music as leaving 'criticism gasping miles behind him'.

Barts Alumni?

The chemical laboratory at St Bartholomew's Hospital (commonly known as Barts) in the City of London has gone down in legend as the location at which Holmes and Watson first met – with, as we have seen, Stamford (Watson's old dresser) as the agent of their coming together.

However, while Watson's association with the institution is straightforward, Holmes's is less so. Watson graduated from its medical school in 1878 but Holmes appeared to be using its facilities under a far looser arrangement. According to Stamford, 'he is well up in anatomy, and he is a first-class chemist; but, as far as I know, he has never taken out any systematic medical classes. His studies are very desultory and eccentric, but he has amassed a lot of out-of-the way knowledge which would astonish his professors.' Who were his professors, and what was their role in his development if he did not attend regular classes? Had he reached some sort of agreement to share the details of any discoveries (such as his haemoglobin test; see next entry) with them in return for a free hand in the laboratory? Certainly, his activities raised eyebrows. Stamford for one was not comfortable when it came to his beating the subjects in the dissecting rooms with a stick. Or had he perhaps used his powers of disguise to persuade the hospital authorities that he was a bona fide student? These are questions we will probably never be able to answer. But Holmes could not have picked a more prestigious medical establishment. The hospital itself was established back in 1123, with the medical school formerly founded in 1843 (although it had been effectively operating since the early part of the century under the guidance of the esteemed surgeon, John Abernethy). A grand Medical School Building was opened in the year that Watson left, and a year earlier, in 1877, a pioneering School of Nursing was opened. No doubt Watson would have enjoyed the opportunity to mingle with the women who studied there but it was his meeting with Holmes that proved most enduringly significant.

A BLOODY BUSINESS

When Watson first encountered Holmes, the detective was celebrating a scientific discovery far ahead of its time. 'I have found a re-agent which is precipitated by haemoglobin, and by nothing else,' he proclaimed. It was, he said, 'the most practical medico-legal discovery for years. Don't you see that it gives us an infallible test for blood stains.' This was by no means an empty claim. It had long been a problem to identify accurately bloodstains, especially when they were not fresh. There was no truly reliable method, for example, of distinguishing a spot of rust from a genuine bloodstain, not to mention telling human from animal blood. As Holmes laboured in the chemistry lab at Bart's, the idea of distinguishing different types of human blood was still decades off. Back in the 1860s, a Swiss chemist called Christian Friedrich Schönbein had noted that if a stain foamed on contact with hydrogen peroxide, it likely contained haemoglobin and so could be assumed to be blood. But it was not an easy test to run. However, according to Holmes, his new method could identify blood in a solution where the proportion of blood was not more than one in a million. This was truly breathtaking stuff.

The Kastle-Meyer Test

In fact, it would not be until 1903 that the real world caught up. In that year, a procedure was developed by the German chemist, Erich Meyer, based on earlier work by an American, Joseph Kastle. The Kastle-Meyer test, as it was known, used phenolphthalein to detect the presence of haemoglobin: the chemical turns bright pink in its presence. At last, the achievement of Holmes could be mirrored in true-life investigations.

A Fine Fellow

Holmes's skills as a chemist were so well established by Conan Doyle that in 2002 the Royal Society of Chemistry decided to bestow an Extraordinary Honorary Fellowship on the detective. The award was symbolically presented to the statue of Holmes that resides outside Baker Street Underground Station. Fittingly, in attendance was a modern-day Fellow of the Society going by the name of John Watson. The Society, established in 1841 as the Chemical Society of London with the aim of generally advancing chemical science, also struck a commemorative silver medal in Holmes's honour. Dr David Giachardi, then chief executive of the Society, commented:

> Our particular interest is his love of chemistry, and the way that he wielded such knowledge for the public good, employing it dispassionately and analytically. He also embodied other personal traits that society seeks in today's law officers – personal rectitude and courage. Last month the Royal Society of Chemistry honoured the achievements of Sir Alec Jeffreys, whose work in the 1980s led to the employment of DNA fingerprinting in criminal detection. But Sir Arthur Conan Doyle, through Holmes, anticipated one hundred and twenty years ago the utilization of chemistry in the battle against crime.

The Last Word in Obscurity

In 'The Bruce-Partington Plans', Watson refers to Holmes having written a monograph on the polyphonic motets of Lassus, which had been printed for private circulation, and 'is said by experts to be the last word upon the subject'. It is difficult to think that it had very much competition. The Lassus in question is Roland de Lassus, a sixteenth-century Flemish composer, whose broad output of work included 516 motets – essentially, complex choral works performed in Latin. The motet is something of an acquired taste. In around 1300, the French musicologist Johannes de Grocheio described the form as something which was 'not to be celebrated in the presence of common people, because they do not notice its subtlety, nor are they delighted in hearing it, but in the presence of the educated and of those who are seeking subtleties in the arts'. For Holmes, there was undoubted beauty to be found in the works of Lassus. 'Do you remember what Darwin says about music?' he once asked Watson. 'He claims that the power of producing and appreciating it existed among the human race long before the power of speech was arrived at.'

THE ENTHUSIASMS OF FRIENDSHIP

The question of whether Holmes's work on the motets was quite as important as Watson suggests is disputed by some Holmesian scholars. As Benjamin Grosbayne has put it: 'As for being "the last word upon the subject," the enthusiasms of friendship must be taken into consideration. Tovey, Koechlin, Jeppesen, Mattieu, Bäumker, Sandberger, E. Van der Straeten and other authorities make no mention of Holmes's monograph.'

The Temple of Food

In two stories ('The Dying Detective' and 'The Illustrious Client') Holmes takes Watson for a bite of something 'nutritious' at Simpsons-in-the-Strand, one of London's foremost dining institutions. A brief résumé of its history suggests why Holmes found it such an appealing spot. It opened in 1828 as a smoking room (no doubt immediately earning it kudos in Holmes's book) but then evolved into a coffee house. During this period, it also became known as the national headquarters of chess. Messengers in top hats would tear around town reporting news of important chess moves as they happened. While Holmes is not known to have been a player himself, it is surely likely that he admired the ultimate game of intellect and strategy. By the 1850s, though, Simpsons had morphed again, this time into a traditional English dining room, famous for its hearty meat dishes. Besides Holmes, its celebrated clientele included Charles Dickens and the prime ministers William Gladstone and Benjamin Disraeli. By the time Holmes and Watson were regulars, it had been subsumed into the grand setting of the Savoy Hotel but maintained its distinct identity. P. G. Wodehouse was another admirer, describing it as 'a restful temple of food'.

Mysteries Within Mysteries

In the canonical stories, there are more than a hundred passing references to cases handled by Holmes about which the details are unknown. Records of at least some of these, it is to be presumed, are sitting in that old, battered dispatch box of Watson's in the vaults of Cox & Co. (see page 61). The little information we are given in many cases leaves more questions than answers, providing a fruitful reserve of inspiration for other authors to create their own Holmes tales. It is impossible for reasons of space to list all of the references here but a taster can be provided. So, here are just fifteen, but each of them pointing towards a lost gem of a story:

- The Abernetty Family (and the depth to which the parsley had sunk into the butter)
- Bert Stevens, the Mild-Mannered Murderer
- The Bogus Laundry Affair
- Colonel Warburton's Madness
- The Colossal Schemes of Baron Maupertuis (Netherland-Sumatra Company)
- The Dundas Separation Case (in which a husband 'had drifted into the habit of winding up every meal by taking out his false teeth and hurling them at his wife')
- The Giant Rat of Sumatra (featuring Matilda Briggs)
- The Madness of Isadora Persano (with a remarkable worm unknown to science)

- The Most Winning Woman (who poisoned three little children)
- The Politician, the Lighthouse and the Trained Cormorant
- The Repulsive Story of the Red Leech and the Terrible Death of Crosby the Banker
- Ricoletti of the Club Foot and his Abominable Wife
- The Singular Affair of the Aluminium Crutch
- The Woman at Margate with no Powder on her Nose
- Wilson, the Notorious Canary-Trainer

Sherlock the Space Cadet?

Everybody knows that Holmes is an intellectual power house, don't they? Well, it turns out that Watson was not quite so convinced of his companion's cerebral brilliance, in their early days at least. Watson's doubts are outlined in an extract from *A Study in Scarlet*, a narrative in which he described the detective's 'ignorance' as being 'as remarkable as his knowledge'. While he described Holmes as strong in the areas of 'sensational literature' ('He appears to know every detail of every horror perpetrated in the century.'), chemistry and anatomy (the latter a field in which he was 'accurate, but unsystematic'), and acknowledged his competence in geology and botany ('Well up in . . . poisons generally. Knows nothing of practical gardening.'), he was utterly dismissive of his basic grasp in other disciplines.

He described as 'nil' Holmes's knowledge of literature (the sensational stuff aside), philosophy and astronomy, while his understanding of politics was but 'feeble'. Holmes particularly shocked Watson by professing to have no knowledge of Copernican theory and the composition of the Solar System. 'That any civilized human being in this nineteenth century should not be aware that the earth travelled round the sun,' pondered Watson, 'appeared to me to be such an extraordinary fact that I could hardly realize it.' Holmes, though, goaded him that now he knew the theory he would do his best to forget it for its lack of practical use to him. 'What the deuce is it to me?' he proclaimed indignantly. While Holmes characterizes himself as a 'brain' with the rest of him 'mere appendix', he was no Renaissance Man-style polymath.

Read-y or Not

As the canon developed, however, Watson's early evaluation of his comrade's academic abilities came to be seen as a little hasty. While Holmes's ignorance of Copernican theory is certainly surprising, the gaps in his knowledge in other areas were surely overestimated. In particular, the canonical stories do not back Watson's assertion that his knowledge of literature was nil. In *The Sign of the Four* alone he twice quotes from that giant of German letters, Johann Wolfgang von Goethe (from two different works, too: Faust and Xenian), commends Jean Paul (the commonly used alias of the German author Johann Paul

Friedrich Richter) and borrows a phrase from François de la Rochefoucauld. Elsewhere, in 'A Case of Identity' he attributes a quote to the fourteenth-century Persian poet Hafiz; in 'The Red-Headed League' he slightly misquotes Gustave Flaubert's letter to George Sand (in which it is suggested 'The man is nothing, the work is everything.'); and in 'The Noble Bachelor' he cites Henry David Thoreau. He was also seen reading a volume of Petrarch on the train to Boscombe Valley. Hardly a man with no interest in literature, then. It is also worth noting that even though he claimed ignorance of the ideas of Copernicus, Holmes was sufficiently versed in astronomy that, in 'The Greek Interpreter', he was able to talk confidently on the 'causes of the changes of the obliquity of the ecliptic'!

By the Book

Despite the aforementioned aspersions cast on Holmes's literary knowledge by Watson, the detective was also a prolific author in his own right. Here is an overview of some of his most important work, each referred to at some point in the canon:

- *The Polyphonic Motets of Lassus*
- *The Practical Handbook of Bee Culture, With Some Observations Upon the Segregation of the Queen*
- *The Book of Life*
- *On the Surface Anatomy of the Human Ear* (for the *Anthropological Journal*).
- *Upon Tattoo Marks*
- *Upon the Dating of Documents by Handwriting Analysis*
- *Upon the Distinction between the Ashes of Various Tobaccos*
- *Upon the Influence of a Trade upon the Form of a Hand*
- *Upon the Subject of Secret Writings*
- *Upon the Tracing of Footsteps (with Some Remarks upon the Uses of Plaster of Paris as a Preserver of Impresses)*

There were several other works in the pipeline too, every bit as esoteric in nature. Whether they were ever completed, we do not know. But what joy to have been able to read *The Chaldean Roots of the Cornish Language*, *The Use of Dogs in Detective Work*, *Malingering* or *The Typewriter and its Relation to Crime*.

Performance of a Lifetime

Holmes has been portrayed on stage, screen and radio by a glorious company of outstanding actors. There is only one, however, who has appeared as Holmes in major

Mum's the Word

Conan Doyle had a close relationship with his mother, Mary, who he always referred to as 'the Ma'am'. She was undoubtedly a resilient woman who overcame many challenges during her lifetime, not least a difficult marriage to Arthur's father. It is to her that we owe 'The Copper Beeches', at least in part. In 1891, Conan Doyle had written to her saying that he was considering finishing Holmes off since he 'takes my mind from better things'. In her reply to him, she implored: 'You won't! You can't! You mustn't!' In January of 1892 he finished the manuscript for 'The Copper Beeches', a story that closely echoed a plot suggestion that the Ma'am had previously made to him. She had told him that he should create a story featuring a girl with 'beautiful golden hair: who kidnapped and her hair shorn should be made to impersonate some other girl for a villainous purpose'. With the exception of Violet Hunter's luxuriant chestnut tresses, he pretty much kept to her suggestions. She in turn had probably been inspired to come up with the plot after reading Charlotte Bronte's *Jane Eyre*. Holmes survived to fight another day, even if Conan Doyle had it in mind to end the story cycle. As he told his mother, Holmes 'lives, thanks to your entreaties, well barely'.

Snake in the Grass

One of the most popular of all the canonical stories (which I shall not name here for fear of spoiling the plot for the uninitiated) pivots around a trained snake. This snake, while a wondrous plot device, nonetheless seems to have little connection to the real world. In the first place, Holmes described the serpent as a 'swamp adder . . . the deadliest snake in India'. Yet there is no such species in India, or indeed on the entire Asian continent, nor was there in Conan Doyle's time. There is a venomous

swamp viper that inhabits areas of East Africa, although the Indian cobra is perhaps a more likely candidate for the snake's true species. The story also makes two rather curious claims about this particular deadly species. First, it suggests it drinks milk, for which there is very little credible supporting scientific evidence, and also that it had been trained to respond to the sound of a whistle. Snakes are to all intents and purposes deaf. Many species are able to detect vibrations and respond to low-frequency noises but the narrative requirement that the snake in question could respond to a whistle blown in a different room stretches credibility to breaking point. Conan Doyle probably found inspiration for this story in an article published in *Cassell's Saturday Journal* in February 1891. It featured the tale of an explorer who had a close encounter with a boa constrictor in West Africa and used a bell-pull to effect his escape. Regardless of its uncertain scientific foundations, Conan Doyle's version of the story packed a bite worthy of even the most aggressive snake.

Smoking Out the Truth

There is an almost universally recognized visual shorthand for Sherlock Holmes – a face in silhouette, sporting a deerstalker and smoking a curved calabash pipe. As we have already seen, the deerstalker was a detail established not by Conan Doyle but by Sidney Paget (see page 24).

Ironically, the calabash pipe also has no place in the original stories. Instead, it is likely that the calabash became a staple of the Holmesian world only when the actor and playwright H. A. Saintsbury utilized it as a prop in his legendary performance as the detective, in the early years of the twentieth century. The canonical stories, meanwhile, specifically mention that his pipe collection included clays, briars and long cherry-woods. Of course, his love of pipes brought about a new phrase in the English language – the 'three-pipe problem', a teaser that is so thorny that it requires an especially extensive period of tobacco consumption to free up the mind. Such was his love of tobacco that he also eagerly consumed cigarettes and cigars, although never with quite the satisfaction with which he would suck upon a pipe.

Tobacco Haze

The 'dense tobacco haze' that surrounded him was so frequently in evidence that smoking is omitted from the narratives of only four of Conan Doyle's sixty stories. No wonder Holmes felt qualified to author a monograph *Upon the Distinction between the Ashes of Various Tobaccos*, of which he identified some 140 variants.

On the Wrong Track

Railways play a recurring role in the canonical stories. Holmes and Watson are regular users of both the London network and cross-country services. Without them, there is every chance that numerous criminals would have escaped justice. But on occasion the railway also served as a backdrop to macabre scenes. Cadogan West was the poor unfortunate in 'The Bruce-Partington Plans', whose body was discovered on the tracks of the London Underground just outside Aldgate Station. The tale was published in 1908 but is set around 1895, when the underground system was barely more than three decades old. The gruesome fate of Cadogan West recalled a real-life crime that rocked the country back in 1864. On 9 July that year, the mortally wounded Thomas Briggs, an elderly banker, was discovered on an embankment next to the tracks somewhere between Bow and Hackney in the east of London. He had been travelling on a train operated by the North London Railway when he was robbed and assaulted just before 10 p.m. A gold watch and watch chain, along with Brigg's black silk chimney pot hat, were taken. Briggs had been beaten around the head with a blunt object that left his carriage covered in blood. He was then thrown from the train. When he was found on the embankment, he was still alive and was initially taken to a public house at nearby Cadogan Terrace, where he succumbed to his injuries. Was Cadogan West's name maybe inspired by this detail of the story? Regardless, what set this crime apart was not merely its brutality but its setting – this was the first murder to be committed on a train in Britain. Police investigations quickly resulted in the finger being pointed at a German tailor called Franz Müller. The suspect fled across the Atlantic with the police in hot pursuit, and he was arrested on American soil in late August. He was found to be in possession of Briggs's watch and also his hat, which Müller had attempted to disguise by reducing its height. Extradited back to Britain, the defendant protested his innocence during a three-day trial but the evidence against him mounted, and he was found guilty. His hanging three months later outside London's Newgate Prison was attended by some 50,000 spectators. Moreover, public perceptions of the railways would never be the same again!

The Wrong Type

'It is a curious thing,' Holmes commented in 'A Case of Identity', 'that a typewriter has really quite as much individuality as a man's handwriting. Unless they are quite new, no two of them write exactly alike. Some letters get more worn than others, and some wear only on one side . . . I think of writing another little monograph some of these days on the typewriter and its relation to crime. It is a subject to which I have devoted some little attention.'

Not for the first time, Holmes proved to be far ahead of his time. The first truly modern typewriter, the Remington Model I, had only come onto the market in the 1870s and Conan Doyle – via Holmes – is believed to be the first to have formally raised the idea that typewriter identification might become a tool of criminal investigators. Where he obtained his knowledge on the subject is not clear.

Levy v. Rust

'A Case of Identity' was published in 1891 but it would be a further two years before such evidence found its way into real world courts. In an 1893 case, Levy v. Rust, an expert witness testified that a series of receipts all featured peculiarities in their printing that were not consistent with them having been produced on the typewriter of the defendant. Sure enough, the judge agreed that the defendant could not have produced the paperwork in question and found in his favour – and so another idea first posited by Holmes found acceptance in the mainstream judicial system.

Getting into Gear

Holmes's world is typically one of hansom cabs and steam engines but in 'His Last Bow', published in 1917 and, in terms of the date when it is set, the latest chronologically (being a tale of 'The War Service of Sherlock Holmes'), the motor car makes its first appearance in the canon. And like buses, having waited so long for one to turn up, you then find two arriving together. Von Bork, the story's German spymaster, zoomed around the place in a '100-horse-power Benz' – a well-chosen vehicle. Karl

Benz, after all, was the epitome of German engineering excellence and a symbol of a country that was confident and international in outlook. It was Benz who invented what is widely regarded as the first practical internal-combustion-engine automobile, for which he received a patent in 1886. Exactly which model Von Bork enjoyed is not certain, but the Benz Company vehicles had a reputation for excellence and power. Meanwhile, Holmes, chauffeured by Watson, travelled in a Ford. Henry Ford's company was American in origin but had been producing vehicles in Manchester since the early 1910s. In fact, by 1913, Ford was by some distance the largest car producer in Britain, churning out Anglicized versions of the original Model A and the astronomically successful Model T. The precise model Holmes drove in is not stated, merely being described as 'little'. The choice of a Ford is perhaps indicative of Conan Doyle's love for all things American, a passion explored on page 176.

Friends in High Places

Only a handful of fictional characters have achieved the global reach of Holmes, and he can claim fans from across the planet and all walks of life. However, he can have had few more powerful fans than Franklin Delano Roosevelt, who occupied the White House from 1933 until 1945. Roosevelt was a passionate admirer of the detective and enjoyed membership of the elite Sherlockian organization, the Baker Street Irregulars. He was even responsible for *A Baker Street Folio: 5 Letters about Sherlock Holmes* – a series of papers prepared for the *Baker Street Journal*, a publication issued by the Baker Street Irregulars. He wrote them during the latter stages of the Second World War, demonstrating that Holmes inadvertently provided a diversion for the leader of the Free World at a crucial moment in world history. The most controversial of Roosevelt's epistles was one that posited that Holmes was in fact an American by birth. According to the presidential thesis, he had been brought up by a father or foster father who inhabited the American underworld, which provided the opportunity for Holmes to be schooled in the theory and practice of criminality. In the letter, written on 18 December 1944, Roosevelt asserted: 'At an early age he felt the urge to do something for mankind. He was too well known in top circles in this country and therefore chose to operate in England. His attributes were primarily American, not English . . .' For all his love of America, surely such a suggestion would have driven Conan Doyle to issue a 'Hands off – he's ours' warning, although the desire to assimilate him into American culture was an undoubted compliment.

HITLER AND THE HOUND

On a more macabre note, it has been suggested that Adolf Hitler was also a rather unexpected fan of Holmes. It is difficult to imagine that the Holmes of, say, 'His

Last Bow', would have been very happy to learn of the German Führer's acclaim. Nonetheless, it is thought that Hitler kept a German film adaptation of *The Hound of the Baskervilles* in his wartime bunker.

You Can't Please Everyone

If Roosevelt was eager to claim Holmes as one of his own, other international leaders have been rather more critical of the detective. Take, for instance, a curious incident in Mao Tse-Tung's China in 1968. With the country in the midst of the Cultural Revolution, the Chinese media reported that a minister of public security had been drummed out of office after attempting to school his agents in Holmes's 'special abilities of detection'. According to a statement issued by the Combined Command Headquarters of Revolutionary Rebels of the Shanghai Public Security Bureau, this represented an unacceptable attempt to mould public security personnel in the image of the 'watchdog of the British bourgeoisie' (a status credited to Holmes, who was seemingly treated as a real human being by the Chinese authorities throughout the affair). There was simply no place in Mao's China for the kind of individualism (not to mention the defence of private property) inherent in Holmes's work. Doubtless driven by similar reservations, Joseph Stalin was another who did not take to the detective – the *Sunday Times* reported in 1950 his 'stubborn refusal

. . . to read any of the Sherlock Holmes adventures'. Yet Holmes has been an enduringly popular figure in Russia, not least during the Soviet era. The publication of *The Hound of the Baskervilles* was received with the same kind of excitement in Moscow as had been evident in London. But perhaps his peak popularity coincided with the phenomenal success of the Russian TV series, *The Adventures of Sherlock Holmes and Dr Watson*. Featuring Vasily Livanov in the main role and running from 1979 to 1986, it commanded huge viewing figures and made a superstar of Livanov. He was even awarded an honorary MBE (Member of the Order of the British Empire) by the British authorities in recognition of his work, and Moscow's statue of Holmes is based upon him.

The Sound of Silence

Very few writers succeed in concocting a form of words so meaningful and evocative that they become absorbed into the fabric of the language. In English, Shakespeare is unrivalled as a coiner of phrases that enter common usage. However, Conan Doyle can claim one or two of his own. Perhaps the most famous is 'the curious incident of the dog in the night time'. The words were originally used in

'Silver Blaze', when Holmes realized the significance of a dog not barking. It is a memorable inversion of the expected order of things – significance usually being attached to that which may be seen or heard or sensed, not to that which is entirely absent. Before long, the phrase became a way of highlighting all manner of significant absences or silences. It has proved a particularly potent verbal grenade for those in the political sphere.

PARLIAMENTARY LANGUAGE

Allusions to 'the curious incident of the dog in the night time' have been made in UK parliamentary debates on at least 35 occasions – while Sherlock Holmes has garnered well over 200 mentions. In 1955, for instance, the British Chancellor of the Exchequer, Rab Butler, launched an attack on the opposition for what he considered omissions in their pre-election manifesto. 'It is rather like Sherlock Holmes and Dr Watson,' he said. 'What was significant about the action of the dog? The dog did not bark.'

The Smoking Gun

Another commonly used phrase for which Conan Doyle and Holmes may legitimately claim the credit is the notion of 'the smoking gun'. Used to mean an item of evidence proving incontrovertible guilt, it can be used in a variety of contexts. In recent history, for instance, political leaders believed that the discovery of weapons of mass destruction would represent 'the smoking gun' necessary to justify the invasion of Iraq. Other examples are less highly charged – from the cat with cream on its whiskers to the accountant with a stash of undocumented receipts or the boy with the football walking away from the broken window – all may be deemed examples of smoking-gun evidence. While Conan Doyle never used that exact phrase himself, he gave a very close approximation in 'The Gloria Scott', published in 1893 but detailing Holmes's first chronological foray into detection. It includes a scene in the cabin of a ship's captain where there lies a body 'with his brains smeared over the chart of the Atlantic . . . while the chaplain stood with a smoking pistol in his hand'. It was this first literary appearance of a 'smoking pistol' that transmuted into the 'smoking gun' of popular parlance.

In the Picture

In 'The Cardboard Box', we gain an intriguing insight into the kind of public figures who stirred the heart of Dr Watson. We learn that he possessed a framed picture of General Charles Gordon, and an unframed one of Henry Ward Beecher. Gordon is perhaps not a surprising choice, having been heralded as one of the great military heroes of the Victorian age. His dramatic career encompassed service in the Crimean War, stints in China and Egypt and a period as Governor-General of the Sudan. Having returned exhausted to Europe at the start of the 1880s, he was re-posted to Khartoum (the Sudanese capital) in 1884 to evacuate British troops and civilians in the face of local rebellion. However, in contravention of his orders, Gordon maintained a small force to counter the rebels, holding off the besieging enemy for the best part of a year. Acclaimed by the public, his masters in London nonetheless resented his ignoring their commands and only supplied a relief force once Khartoum had fallen and Gordon was dead. He was the sort of courageous maverick, regarded by the public virtually as a martyr, who would have appealed to Watson the steadfast military man. By contrast, Henry Ward Beecher was a less predictable choice. A noted social reformer who campaigned hard for the abolition of slavery, he was sent to Europe by Abraham Lincoln to raise funds for the Union forces in the American Civil War. This was probably when Watson encountered him, drawn to his reputation for moral rectitude. However, in 1875 Ward Beecher became embroiled in a notorious adultery trial and while he was ultimately acquitted of all charges, it did his good name enduring harm. It is possible Conan Doyle shoehorned him into his story as an oblique reference to the marital infidelity that forms an important aspect of the plot. Given the uncertainty over Watson's own marital situation, it is intriguing that the doctor should have so admired a man himself accused of extramarital shenanigans.

The Adventure of the Two Collaborators

Today, J. M. Barrie is best known as the creator of Peter Pan, but even before that he was among the foremost authors of his age. He was also a close friend of Conan Doyle, and created some of the earliest Holmes pastiches. The two met while Conan Doyle was working at *The Idler* magazine and their friendship was consolidated through a mutual love of cricket that saw them play for the same side. Barrie's first Holmes effort came in 1891, when the character was enjoying his first flush of success in *The Strand*. That November, just four months after Conan Doyle had debuted the detective in the short-story format, 'My Evening with Sherlock Holmes' appeared in the *Speaker* magazine, its author uncredited. It was a frivolous and affectionate skit in which the author declares: 'To my annoyance (for I hate to hear anyone praised except myself) Holmes's cleverness in, for instance, knowing by glancing at you what you had for dinner last Thursday, has delighted press and public, and so I felt it was time to take him down a peg.' Then, in 1892, Barrie was struck down by a bout of bronchitis aggravated by anxiety at the lack of progress he was making on a commission – a booklet for an operetta called *Jane Annie; or, the Good Conduct Prize*. Conan Doyle visited him and agreed to help him complete the project. To show his gratitude, Barrie wrote 'The Two Collaborators', which was said to have been written on the flyleaf of one of Barrie's novels, *A Window in Thrums*. In the story, Holmes and Watson attempt to get to the bottom of the failure of an opera that Watson has composed. The third and final pastiche, 'The Late Sherlock Holmes' was published in the *St James's Gazette* on 29 December 1893, just a few weeks after Holmes had apparently met his end in 'The Final Problem'. In Barrie's take, Watson is accused of having had a hand in his old companion's demise before (somewhat prophetically) it is discovered that all is not what it seems. If imitation is the ultimate form of flattery, how much more satisfying for Conan Doyle must it have been that a friend and talent such as Barrie was behind it.

Never the Twain

One leading literary light who was rather more ambiguous in his attitude to Holmes was Samuel Langhorne Clemens, better known by his pen name of Mark Twain. In 1902, Twain – author of such classics as *The Adventures of Tom Sawyer* and *The Adventures of Huckleberry Finn* – produced *A Double-Barrelled Detective Story*. It appeared shortly after Conan Doyle had unleashed *The Hound of the Baskervilles* onto the world. Twain's tale, set in the American West, was an acerbic parody of the detective fiction genre of which Conan Doyle was at the forefront. For Twain, Conan Doyle's stories were just too perfectly formed, and Holmes too superhumanly analytical. So, in this story, we get a murderous character by the name of Fetlock Jones, who just happens to be the nephew of Sherlock Holmes. When it is discovered that Holmes himself has arrived on the scene, the 'village was electrified with an immense sensation'. But Jones is rather more sanguine about his relation's abilities: 'Anybody that knows him the way I do knows he can't detect a crime except where he plans it all out beforehand and arranges the clues and hires some fellow to commit it according to instruction.' Sure enough, Holmes draws quite the wrong conclusions from the evidence before him, despite going through a quite logical process of deduction. It was to all intents and purposes, one great author cocking a snook at another.

Monkeying Around

'The Creeping Man', published in 1923, has the ability to split Holmes fans. To some it is the kind of exuberant narrative that marks out Conan Doyle's genius. To others, the story of a man who undergoes something of a personality change in pursuit of reversing the effects of aging is considered a pot-boiler bit of sci-fi nonsense. Yet it has perhaps a little more scientific veracity than it is sometimes credited with. Or at the very least, it had a legitimate basis in real-life scientific endeavour, even if that endeavour was subsequently discredited and ridiculed. From the late nineteenth century, there had been a school of thought that the effects of aging might be stalled by injecting material from the testicles of various animals, among them dogs. A French scientist of Russian extraction, Serge Voronoff, took things on a stage further when he began grafting testicular tissue from monkeys on to humans. Claiming remarkable results in boosting wellbeing and restoring vigour, by the 1920s he was able to charge private clients large amounts of money for his work. Small volumes of baboon and chimp tissue were surgically inserted into the patient's scrotum in a bid to stave off senility and prompt physical and mental rejuvenation.

No More Baboons

With sad predictability, it became apparent over time that Vornoff's work brought none of the benefits that he claimed. The 'famous doctor who inserts monkeyglands in millionaires', as the poet E. E. Cummings once described him, found himself falling out of favour so that by the time he died in 1951, he was considered little more than a crank. But when Conan Doyle was composing 'The Creeping Man', Voronoff was still a man on the up.

Following in the Footsteps

· ·

Perhaps the classic caricature of Holmes depicts him inspecting footprints in the dust through a magnifying glass. As with many clichés, it is rooted in truth, for the examination of footsteps plays a part in a great many of the canonical investigations. Indeed, Holmes said of the art of tracing footsteps: 'There is no branch of detective science which is so important and so much neglected' and duly wrote a monograph on 'the tracing of footsteps, with some remarks upon the uses of plaster of Paris as a preserver of impresses'. In 1953, Conan Doyle's sons, Adrian and Denis, cited that paper as evidence that their father had invented the use of plaster of Paris for preserving footprints – another proof, they suggested, of their thesis that the 'police systems of the modern world are founded on the new ideas in criminology, expressed by our father in his detective stories . . .' While Holmes may have innovated the plaster of Paris technique, some years earlier police ensnared a suspect by getting her to reproduce footprints found at a crime scene in the medium of cows' blood. This footprint evidence played a vital part in the sensational trial of Jessie McLachlan for the murder of her friend, Jessie McPherson, in Glasgow in 1862. The victim, a domestic servant, was found hacked to death with a meat cleaver and suspicion initially fell on her master's aged father. However, the court was presented with the evidence that it was McLachlan who was responsible for producing a series of bloody footprints close to the victim's body. She was subsequently convicted of murder and served out a long sentence.

THROUGH A LENS DARKLY

The Jessie McLachlan case was also the first British trial to admit crime scene photographic evidence. However, it was several more decades before such evidence was commonplace in the British judicial system. Scotland Yard, for instance, only employed specialist photographers from 1901, simply using regular commercial photographers to snap crime scenes up until that point. For a man so generally ahead of his time when it came to forensic techniques, Holmes himself was peculiarly slow to pick up on this trend. It was only in 'The Lion's Mane', published in 1926 but set circa 1907, that he gave a nod to the power of photography. Producing an enlarged print of a victim's wounds, he declared: 'This is my method in such cases.'

'You certainly do things thoroughly, Mr Holmes,' his companion said.

'I should hardly be what I am if I did not,' he shot back. It was a curiously disingenuous exchange, given that there is no evidence that he ever produced another crime scene image in this way. Of course, there might be reams of photos locked away in Watson's old tin dispatch box. Or maybe Holmes was just hoping to gloss over the fact that in this one area at least, he was a little behind the times.

On the Shoulders of Giants

Holmes is the most recognizable of all fictional detectives and Conan Doyle stands almost unrivalled among the pantheon of crime fiction authors. Arguably the only other author who might claim to be his equal in terms of global and enduring popularity is Agatha Christie. Her breakthrough novel, *The Mysterious Affair at Styles*, was published in 1920 so there was a brief period in which her career and Conan Doyle's overlapped. She did graciously acknowledge the debt she owed to her literary progenitor. Reflecting in her autobiography on what sort of detective she wanted to write about, she said: 'There was Sherlock Holmes, the one and only – I should never be able to emulate him.' Emulate or not, she decided her hero needed 'a grand name – one of those names that Sherlock Holmes and his family had. Who was it his brother had been? Mycroft Holmes.' Sure enough, Hercule Poirot was born. Moreover, as the series developed, she came to realize she was subconsciously echoing Holmes, writing – as she put it – 'in the Sherlock Holmes tradition – eccentric detective, stooge assistant [Captain Hastings], with a Lestrade-type Scotland Yard detective, Inspector Japp – and now I added a "human foxhound", Inspector Giraud, of the French police.' In the 1963 novel, *The Clocks*, she even allowed Poirot to pay personal tribute to Conan Doyle. In the Belgian's words:

It is the author, Sir Arthur Conan Doyle, that I salute. These tales of Sherlock Holmes are in reality far-fetched, full of fallacies and most artificially contrived. But the art of the writing – ah, that is entirely different. The pleasure of the language, the creation above all of that magnificent character, Dr Watson. Ah, that was indeed a triumph.

Another pair of her heroes – this time, Tommy and Tuppence – got in on the act in *The Case of the Missing Lady* (1972) when they tried to pass themselves off as Holmes and Watson. The shadow of the great detective and the good doctor loomed large indeed.

The Curious Incident of the Glove

Conan Doyle did not have much to say on the record about Christie's creations but he did play an intriguing cameo role in the saga of her eleven-day disappearance in 1926. Asked whether he might be able to assist the enquiry, he took one of Christie's gloves for inspection by a medium with whom he was familiar through his psychical research. Needless to say, their experiments on the glove yielded nothing of much value.

A Wimsey-cal View

Christie was not the only one of the Golden Age crime writers to fall for Holmes. Dorothy L. Sayers – most famous as the creator of Lord Peter Wimsey, who debuted in *Whose Body?* in 1923 – was something of a superfan. An inaugural member of the Sherlock Holmes Society, she combined her feel for crime writing and her prodigious academic abilities (she was a graduate of Oxford's Somerville College) to produce a series of much-loved essays on Holmes, which she composed between 1928 and 1946. She wrote a treatise, for instance, on the relationship between the tales of Holmes and those of Dupin, and another that sought to accurately timetable the events depicted in 'The Red-Headed League'. More famously, she investigated the mystery over Watson's wives and the question of his first and middle name. And in 1954, she wrote a radio play for the BBC's 'A Tribute to Sherlock Holmes on the Occasion of His 100th Birthday'. Called *A Young Lord Peter Consults Sherlock Holmes*, it brought Wimsey (in a youthful form) and Holmes (in his dotage) together for the first time. It would prove to be the last Wimsey piece she would ever write and it was doubtless a fitting way for him to exit the scene.

A SIDNEY SUSSEX FELLOW

Dorothy Sayers also made a strong case that Holmes was a graduate of the University of Cambridge (specifically

Sidney Sussex College) based on some vague references in 'The Adventure of the Gloria Scott' and 'The Adventure of the Musgrave Ritual', mixed with a good dollop of imaginative speculation.

A Clubable Fellow

Sherlock's brother Mycroft was famously described as among the 'most unclubable men in town'. Nor was Sherlock given to an excess of sociability, yet a raft of clubs and societies have sprung up in his honour over the years. The first one in the UK appeared in 1934 and owed much to Dorothy L. Sayers. She and a number of now legendary Holmesians – among them Ronald Knox (see page 92) and the American journalist and author, Vincent Starrett – met for a sherry party hosted by the Scottish writer and broadcaster, A. G. Macdonell. The gathering declared themselves the Sherlock Holmes Society and sporadic dinners were held before the organization was wound up in 1938. Meanwhile, across the Atlantic, Starrett was also involved in the creation of the Baker Street Irregulars, which had its inaugural meeting in January 1934. The original membership included Christopher Morley, a newspaper man who had previously co-founded

The Saturday Review of Literature. He contributed a regular column to that publication, often discoursing on Holmes and related subjects so that he had come to be regarded as Ronald Knox's counterpart in America. The Baker Street Irregulars held their first annual dinner at the end of 1934 and counted among the guests William Gillette, Frederic Dorr Steele (Holmes's principal illustrator in the US) and even Gene Tunney, better known as a world heavyweight boxing champion. The Irregulars took firm root and continue to thrive to the current day. Back in Britain, though, it was not until 1951 that the embers of the Sherlock Holmes Society were reignited. That year, a Holmes-themed exhibition was put on as part of the Festival of Britain. Its organizers decided to resurrect the Society too, renaming it the Sherlock Holmes Society of London. Today, it is thought that there are at least several hundred societies throughout the world dedicated to the detective, although the rise of social media means there are probably many more ad hoc groupings as well.

Identifying Irene

Perhaps the most memorable female character in the entire canon is Irene Adler, who appears in 'A Scandal in Bohemia'. An American-born opera singer with an exotic personal life and 'the face of the most beautiful of women and the mind of the most resolute of men', she became known by Holmes as simply 'the woman'. Where few managed ever to get one over on the great detective, she comprehensively matched him move for move. It has been long suggested that the inspiration for the character of Adler was the famed actress and lover of Edward, Prince of Wales, Lily Langtry. Born in 1853, Langtry came from the small island of Jersey (a UK dependency), while Adler came from across the Atlantic in New Jersey. Like Adler, Langtry was famous for both her looks and talents as a performer, winning acceptance into elevated social circles. The married Langtry was linked to a number of aristocratic paramours, but it was her relationship with Edward, which began in 1877, that garnered most attention, especially after she was introduced to Queen Victoria. However, by 1880 she was pregnant by another man and involved with several others, so that her relationship with the prince gradually faded. She led quite the life of drama and intrigue which must surely have come to the notice of Conan Doyle, and she is undoubtedly a good candidate for the Adler blueprint.

ALTERNATIVE WOMEN

However, there are other contenders for the original of 'the woman'. Prominent among them are Lola Montez – an Irish-born performer renowned as a Spanish dancer who became the lover of King Ludwig I of Bavaria – and Ludmilla Stubel – the opera-dancing lover and, later, wife of Archduke Johann Salvator of Austria.

Arise, Sir Sherlock

In 'The Three Garridebs' (published in 1925), Watson noted: 'I remember the date [June 1902] very well, for it was in the same month that Holmes refused a knighthood for services which may perhaps some day be recorded.' The choice of month was a considered one for it was then that Conan Doyle himself was offered his knighthood. The honour, however, did not sit easily with the author. He received it not for creating Holmes nor for any of his other fictional work, but in recognition of his efforts to bolster support for the Boer War in a pamphlet entitled 'The War in South Africa: Its Causes and Conduct'. Conan Doyle had been brought up by his mother to admire the chivalric tradition and he had avidly consumed tales of King Arthur and his Round Table. This childhood fascination went on to find expression in works such as *The White Company* and *Sir Nigel*. But he was not sure that honours and titles served much purpose in the modern world. He regarded them as – outside of military and diplomatic circles at least – 'the badge of the provincial mayor'. It came down to a question of pride. As he told his mother: 'Fancy Rhodes or Chamberlain or Kipling doing such a thing! And why should my standards be lower than theirs.' Nonetheless, in June 1902 he dined with Edward VII and from then felt he could not reject the honour without seeming rude. He was at least buoyed by the congratulations of his contemporaries, among them H. G. Wells, who told him that 'none . . . combine so happily as you do a large part in the public mind with the genuine respect of those who care keenly for literature'. But Conan Doyle refused to be styled as 'Sir Arthur' in his literary works, arguing: 'I am A. Conan Doyle without any trimmings and will so remain.' Holmes's rejection in June 1902 was surely Conan Doyle living vicariously through his creation.

Keeping It in the Family

Arthur Conan Doyle was not the only Conan Doyle to write stories about Sherlock Holmes. In the 1950s, his youngest son, Adrian, got in on the act, too. In the mid-1940s, he worked with John Dickson Carr, a celebrated mystery writer, on what became a lauded biography of his father. In the early 1950s the two combined again to author a series of short stories faithful in style and tone to the original tales, each based on references in the canonical stories to undocumented cases. With the exception of one story first published in *Life* magazine, the tales appeared first in *Colliers*, which had been the original publisher of most of the canonical stories in the US. Their twelve stories were then released as a collection in 1954. It met with only moderate success although the Conan Doyle name assured them a certain place in the Holmesian landscape. There were also rumours that the writing partnership was not always a happy one.

The New Tales

Adrian's stories were entitled as follows: 'The Gold Hunter', 'The Wax Gamblers', 'The Highgate Miracle', 'The Black Baronet', 'The Sealed Room', 'Foulkes Rath', 'The Abbas Ruby', 'The Dark Angels', 'The Two Women', 'The Deptford Horror' and 'The Red Widow'.

Putting Your Finger on It

It is not too much of a stretch to say that Holmes was the foremost exponent of fingerprint evidence working in Britain at the end of the nineteenth century. It is another example of him leading and real-world detectives following. William James Herschel, a British colonial administrator in India, is often credited with being the first person to systematically use fingerprints as a method of identification. Indeed, he argued for their administrative use in the Indian courts as early as 1877. Previously, it had been customary for criminals to simply disappear and slip through the net for years at a time with no reliable means of documenting their identity. Then, in 1880, a Scot called Henry Faulds first proposed the use of fingerprints in criminal investigations, by comparing the prints of a suspect to those found at a crime scene. Francis Galton carried out ground-breaking analysis of prints from the early 1890s, cataloguing different characteristics and calculating the odds of two people having identical prints at something approaching one in 64 billion. In 1892, Argentina opened the first fingerprint bureau for law enforcement officers, but it would be a further nine years before Scotland Yard followed suit. Not until 1905 was a murderer first convicted in the British courts on the basis of fingerprint evidence (brothers named Stratton were convicted of killing a shopkeeper and his wife in Deptford, London, thanks to a print found on a cashbox). Yet Holmes had routinely used fingerprint evidence since the early 1890s, utilizing the technique in seven cases – perhaps most notably to ensnare the culprit in 'The Norwood Builder'.

Take That!

Holmes might be best known for the power of his brain, but he was pretty handy at combat sports, too. He stated his preference for fencing, and claimed in 'The Solitary Cyclist' that he had '. . . some proficiency in the good old British sport of boxing'. We know, too, that he once went three rounds with McMurdo the prize-fighter from *The Sign of the Four*, while in 'The Yellow Face' Watson described him as 'one of the finest boxers of his weight that I have ever seen'. Holmes put those skills on display in 'The Solitary Cyclist' when he boxed the ears of a rogue called Woodley, who had to be sent 'home in a cart'.

Baritsu or Bartitsu

During his legendary encounter with Moriarty at the Reichenbach Falls, Holmes turned not to boxing but to his notable abilities in baritsu – a 'Japanese system of wrestling, which has more than once been very useful to me'. There is just one problem with his claim. There is no such sport, nor any indication that it ever existed. It is likely Conan Doyle was deliberately or accidentally mis-rendering Bartitsu, a form of self-defence containing elements of boxing, jujitsu, kickboxing and stick-fighting. It was the brainchild of an Englishman, Edward Barton-Wright, who introduced it in Britain around 1898 having lived for several years in Japan. It was gaining some traction among enthusiasts at the time when Conan Doyle was writing of Holmes's encounter with Moriarty, although it had not yet been invented when their fight was supposed to have taken place. But then, Holmes always was ahead of his time.

A Dog-ged Pursuit

In 'The Creeping Man', Holmes claimed to be giving serious thought to writing a monograph on the use of dogs in the work of the detective. He could claim a number of canine successes in his own career. In particular, he used 'an ugly, long-haired, lop-eared creature, half spaniel and half lurcher, brown-and white in colour, with a very clumsy waddling gait' called Toby in *The Sign of the Four*. He was, Holmes said, 'a queer mongrel, with a most amazing power of scent. I would rather have Toby's help than that of the whole detective force of London'. Then there was Pompey in 'The Missing Three-Quarter', 'the pride of the local draghounds – no very great flier, as his build will show, but a staunch hound on a scent'. The advantage Holmes obtained from his dog companions was in marked contrast to the experiences of the London police in the late Victorian period. During the Jack the Ripper investigation of 1888, the employment of two bloodhounds called Burgho and Barnaby was a fairly unmitigated disaster. It was after the slaughter of Elizabeth Stride and Catherine Eddowes at the end of September that there was a call for dogs to be put on the scent of the killer. Burgho and Barnaby were duly trialled for a permanent position on the force, having been obtained from a bloodhound breeder in Yorkshire called Edwin Brough. While the dogs proved effective at tracking scents over long distances in practice exercises, the experiment soon started coming undone. With the

Ripper briefly ceasing his activities, there was no fresh scent to pursue. Then the press inaccurately reported that the dogs had got lost in the London fog just as they were being summoned to an assignment. In fact, they were on a training session on Tooting Common when the call came from a distant part of the city, so it was actually London's geography that prevented them from attending. By the end of October, Brough had taken his dogs back after receiving no official indication that they were wanted long term. But word of their departure had not spread widely among the police, so when Mary Kelly fell victim to the Ripper in early November, the dogs were again summoned (this being the ideal opportunity for them to prove what they could do) and the crime scene was left undisturbed for fully two hours before it emerged that the hounds would not be making an appearance after all. Several years later, Brough would suggest that the Ripper deliberately paused his slaughter while the dogs were operating in the city. Whether that is true or not, we shall never know. But how many lives might have been saved had Pompey and Toby been on the murderer's trail rather than Burgho and Barnaby.

Ripper Yarns

It was the crime that shocked a nation and has resonated down the generations. Jack the Ripper prowled the East End of London from 1888 until perhaps 1891 and was responsible for the brutal murders of at least five women and maybe as many as eleven. They were slayings for which no one was ever ultimately held responsible. As we have seen elsewhere in this book, Conan Doyle eagerly seized upon real-life crimes to inform the Holmes stories. However, the absence of any Ripper-inspired narratives, or even allusions, are striking in a 'curious incident of the dog in the night time' sort of way. Several authors and film-makers have subsequently matched the detective against the Ripper, with varying degrees of success – the movies *A Study in Terror* and *Murder by Decree* are two of the more notable examples. Yet Conan Doyle steered clear of the subject entirely. The reason is perhaps to be found in an observation Holmes made in 'The Naval Treaty': '. . . the most difficult crime to track is the one which is purposeless.' Holmes's genius relied on an ability to spot the detail that did not fit with the expected norm – the snag in the fabric that when tugged could unravel a whole case – along with a deep understanding of human motivations (among them, revenge, passion and greed) that belied his reputation for being unempathetic. In a case like that of the Ripper, though, the crimes lacked any clear rationale – there was no pre-existing relationship between killer and victim in each case, no sane motivation to explain the slaughter. They were instead crimes that suggest the kind of psychopathological or sociopathological malfunctioning that did not ever find a place in the canon. Nonetheless, Conan Doyle did undertake some exploration of the Ripper murders himself – but he made precious little headway. The case did not seem to grab his imagination in the way of the

Edalji or Slater cases (see pages148 and 162), where clear lines of evidence could be examined and evaluated.

THE BLACK MUSEUM

In late 1892 – when the Ripper murders were still fresh in the collective memory – Conan Doyle was shown around Scotland Yard's 'invitation only' museum (known as the Black Museum). There he was shown a letter that purported to be from the Ripper. Why, Doyle asked, had a facsimile not been made and publicized around the world – as he was sure Holmes would have done – in the hope that someone, somewhere would recognize the handwriting? Then, in 1903 or 1904, he was taken on a tour of the Whitechapel streets that had provided the backdrop for the Ripper's violence, with an officer who had worked on the case showing him around. All to no avail, though. Jack the Ripper was simply not the kind of quarry that Holmes or Conan Doyle were well adapted to stalk.

A Bad Habit

There is a popular misconception that Holmes was addicted to opium. He was not. He was famously spotted by Watson in a Limehouse opium den in 'The Man with the Twisted

Lip', but that was in the interests of an investigation and he was quick to reassure Watson that he had not taken up the evil O. He was, though, an inveterate user of cocaine and an occasional user of morphine. In *The Sign of the Four*, for example, there is the most astonishing scene of Holmes – for want of a better phrase – shooting-up. A story published in 1890 and set a couple of years earlier, there he is with a bottle of his favoured seven-per-cent solution of cocaine and a hypodermic syringe extracted from a neat morocco case. His long, white fingers are described as 'nervous' and his 'sinewy forearm and wrist' are 'all dotted and scarred with innumerable puncture-marks'. Only with the hit is he able to sink back into his 'velvet-lined armchair with a long sigh of satisfaction'. The fact of the matter is that at this stage in Holmes's career, cocaine was still a relatively new and little understood drug.

THE ORIGINAL COKE

It had only been in 1884 that the Austrian opthalmologist, Karl Koller, first heralded cocaine as a wonder anaesthetic. His friend Sigmund Freud was another enthusiast, publishing a celebratory scientific paper ('On Coca') that same year. Two years later, in the US, John Pemberton would use the coca leaf from which the drug is derived in his initial formulation for Coca-Cola.

Holmes's addiction probably began when cocaine was still regarded as a legitimate means of bringing peace of mind and inducing positive physiological effects. It was not long, however, before serious doubts as to its safeness arose. Freud, for example, had introduced it to a friend who soon began suffering the symptoms of chronic addiction, leading ultimately to his death in 1891. By the end of the 1880s, few were labouring under the illusion that it was the panacea it had once been assumed to be. Watson was certainly well attuned to its dangers and even Holmes acknowledged: 'I suppose that its influence is physically a bad one.' Nonetheless, he continued to use for several more years, although with diminishing regularity. By the time of 'The Missing Three-Quarter' (published 1904 but set in the mid-1890s), thanks in no small part to Watson's prolonged intervention, Holmes had stopped using, saving him from 'that drug mania which had threatened once to check his remarkable career'.

A Gambling Man? You Bet

Think of Dr Watson and the chances are you imagine a figure of doughty dependability and straightforwardness. But Watson had his demons as much as the next person. He may have scolded Holmes for his chemical vices, but his own life was far from vice-free. In particular, Conan Doyle hinted that the doctor had something of a gambling problem. Take, for example, an exchange between Holmes and Watson in 'Shoscombe Old Place' – a story that pivots around one man's desire to win the famous Epsom Derby race. 'By the way, Watson, you know something of racing?' Holmes asks. 'I ought to,' comes the reply. 'I pay for it with about half my wound pension.' Then there is a curious detail in 'The Dancing Men'. Watson has been invited to make an investment but Holmes concludes that he is not keen to since 'Your cheque book is locked in my drawer, and you have not asked for the key.' Why on earth should Holmes be guardian of Watson's money? Because, simply, he cannot be trusted with it himself – the result of his penchant for gambling. Gaming is a recurrent motif in the Holmes stories. Besides 'Shoscombe Old Place', horse racing is also central to 'Silver Blaze', while in other tales assorted characters are shown to have fallen on hard times as a result of betting – among them the ancient Roylott family in 'The Speckled Band' and Sir George Burnwell in 'The Beryl Coronet'.

VICTORIAN GAMBLERS

For the ostensibly strait-laced Victorians, gambling represented a serious threat to the social fabric. Generally regarded as a vice of the lower classes (one contemporary commentator claimed that it blossomed amid the 'ignorance of servants and others of the least intelligent class'), in truth it claimed many upper-class victims, too. For instance, in the mid-nineteenth century a certain Squire Osbaldeston

– a Member of Parliament and celebrated sportsman who excelled as a jockey, rower and cricketer – built up gambling debts in excess of £200,000 (some £2 million in modern money) and had to sell his estates before dying in poverty in 1866. By the time Holmes was at work, the bookmaker was regarded as among the lowliest figures in society. It is somewhat surprising that Conan Doyle should then inflict a gambling problem upon the otherwise upright Watson, but it certainly makes for a far more nuanced character.

Beastly Behaviour

In 'Silver Blaze', Holmes detects a subtle pattern of animal mutilations inflicted by scalpel. That story was published in 1892 but fifteen years later Conan Doyle would find himself fighting the case of a man accused of much more gruesome animal butchery. George Edalji was brought up in a village, Great Wyrley, not far from Birmingham. His mother was an English woman and his father a Parsee Indian who had become a Church of England vicar. It was an unorthodox background and George experienced a good deal of racial intolerance growing up. Nonetheless, he was a bright boy who applied himself to his studies and looked set to prosper. Then, about the time that 'Silver Blaze' first appeared in *The Strand*, he was accused of sending a series of disturbing, anonymous letters around his village. Eleven years later, Great Wyrley experienced a spate of grisly attacks on horses, sheep and cows, in which the animals were cut along their stomachs with a sharp knife and left to bleed to death. More anonymous letters flew around the town, naming Edalji – who by then had established a successful legal practice – as the culprit. He was arrested, found guilty and sentenced to seven years of hard labour. Yet the evidence against him was scant. An expert witness who had accused him of being the author of those earlier abusive letters was discredited, soil samples that were used to link him to the crime scenes were flawed and, perhaps most pertinently, the mutilations continued even after his conviction. The case garnered significant attention and, under pressure from campaigners convinced there had been a miscarriage of justice, Edalji was freed after three years. However, he was not pardoned and was thus unable to continue to work as a solicitor. Conan Doyle heard of the case in late 1906 and was soon convinced of Edalji's innocence. Then, early the following year, he went to meet Edalji in person. Edalji was already in the hotel lounge designated for their interview, reading a newspaper when Conan Doyle arrived. The author at once realized from Edalji's mode of reading that he had terrible eyesight – so bad, he was sure, that the idea that he could carry out the finely executed mutilations in the dead of night of which he was accused did not stand up. Conan Doyle took to the press to fight Edalji's corner and within a few months he was cleared by a specially assembled government commission. This meant he could at last resume his career in the law. His case was also instrumental in pushing forward plans for a Court of Criminal Appeal, which was established before the year was out.

The Best Man for the Job

Early in *The Hound of the Baskervilles*, James Mortimer tells Holmes that he has consulted him because 'you are the second highest expert in Europe'.

'May I inquire who has the honour to be first?' Holmes asked, not unreasonably.

'To the man of precisely scientific mind,' came the reply, 'the work of Monsieur Bertillon must always appeal strongly.'

It was by no means an unreasonable claim as Alphonse Bertillon developed new investigative methods adopted throughout the world around the time that Holmes was active. Holmes even acknowledged his greatness, expressing enthusiastic admiration in 'The Naval Treaty' for the 'French savant'. So just what did Bertillon do? His greatest contribution was to revolutionize methods of criminal identification and cataloguing through the application of anthropometry (the scientific study of the proportions and measurements of the body). Born in 1853, he became an officer in the French police force and soon recognized the deficiencies in the existing system of identification, which was based on names linked to photographic images. As a result, it was all too easy for recidivist miscreants to assume a different name or superficially alter their appearance and so escape the clutches of the law for years at a time. Alongside photographs of arrested felons, Bertillon introduced a record of numerous physical features, among them the length and breadth of the head, and lengths of the left foot, the forearm and the middle finger – all features that could not be easily altered. He also took account of the shapes of facial features and noted specific individual characteristics including tattoos and scars. Furthermore, he helped develop the standardized 'mugshot', with views taken from the front and side. The so-called Bertillon system was not without its flaws – it was, for instance, best suited to cataloguing fully grown males, although in reality that encompassed the majority of serious criminals – but it was a major step forward. Before long it was rolled out throughout Europe and the Americas. Only with significant advances in fingerprint technology – an area to which Bertillon himself contributed – was it eventually superseded.

FOOTPRINTS AND BALLISTICS

Bertillon also oversaw a number of other forensic advances that Holmes would doubtless have regarded with a mixture of appreciation and mild envy. For example, he developed means of footprint preservation using plastic compounds, pioneered new methods of crime scene photography and recording, progressed our understanding of ballistics and even invented a bit of kit that could measure the amount of force used in cases of breaking-and-entering. The head of his profession, with Holmes a close second? It is a bold claim but a case can certainly be made.

Away with the Fairies

Holmes – with his reputation for unshakeable rationalism – was not one to give much credence to the idea of the supernatural. In 'The Devil's Foot', he flatly refused 'to admit diabolical intrusions into the affairs of men'. It came as a huge surprise to some fans, then, when in the 1920s Conan Doyle took up his pen to suggest that the world was in possession of photographic evidence of the existence of fairies. It was in 1920 that Conan Doyle, whose belief in Spiritualism was already well established (see page 164), learned of the existence of the said photos. They had been taken by two young Yorkshire girls, Elsie Wright and her cousin Frances Griffiths, and purported to show fairies

spotted in the village of Cottingley back in 1917. Doyle was at first sceptical but his friend, Edward L. Gardner – a member of the mystical Theosophical Society – was convinced. Whatever they were, Conan Doyle came to believe that there was something deeply mysterious about the figures captured in the images. When it turned out that the girls had taken more fairy photos in 1920, Conan Doyle seems to have been swept up in the excitement. He wrote an article about the fairy pictures for *The Strand* in December 1920, which led to him being deluged with more photographs, some claiming to be further authentic images of fairies and others claiming to show how easily they could have been faked. Conan Doyle remained resolute, claiming that the legitimacy of the Cottingley fairies pictures had yet to be undermined. In 1922, he wrote an account of the entire affair called *The Coming of the Fairies*. In its conclusion, he said that there was sufficient evidence 'already available to convince any reasonable man that the matter is not one which can be readily dismissed, but that a case actually exists which up to now has not been shaken in the least degree by any of the criticism directed against it'. It was only in the 1980s that Elsie Wright admitted the photos were a hoax after all, constructed in part from pictures of fairies cut from the 1915 edition of *Princess Mary's Gift Book* (to which, ironically, Conan Doyle had been a contributor). Frances Griffiths, however, claimed the authenticity of one of the photos until her dying day. Conan Doyle never lost his faith in the pictures.

THE LITTLE PEOPLE

Conan Doyle's father (see page 47) had been well known for his numerous illustrations of fairies and elves which were produced in Arthur's childhood – so perhaps the Cottingley photos tapped into a fascination which had long been harboured in Conan Doyle's psyche. Diabolical intrusions, indeed.

A Man of Pseudo-Science

As is evident from the pages of this book, Holmes often operated at the cutting edge of science. Yet, curiously, he found time to indulge in one branch that had already been widely discredited – that of phrenology, or the study of cranial anatomy in order to identify specific character traits. Most famously, in 'The Blue Carbuncle', Holmes examines a hat to establish the dimensions of the skull of its wearer, from which analysis he attempts to discern the wearer's intellect. In 'The Final Problem', meanwhile, Holmes finds himself the object of phrenological investigation when Moriarty tells him: 'You have less frontal development than I should have expected' (a snide attempt to belittle Holmes's intellectual capabilities). The discipline of phrenology was the creation of the German-born physiologist, Franz Joseph Gall (1758–1828). His single most important work was *The Anatomy and Physiology of the Nervous System in General, and of the Brain in Particular, with Observations upon the possibility of ascertaining the several Intellectual and Moral Dispositions of Man and Animal* (1819). In it, he laid out his thesis that the brain is the organ of the mind and consists of numerous regions, each with a specific function that influences character: the larger the region, the more powerful its function. Moreover, he argued, the skull develops so that studying the cranial structure can indicate the size of specific components of the brain. His work was for a time extremely influential. It was also regularly hijacked by those who wished to put forward their own theories of racial superiority. In the field of criminology, meanwhile, the Italian Cesare Lombroso developed Gall's ideas as he sought to prove a link between physical characteristics and inherent criminality. But as early as the 1840s, there was a growing body of scientific evidence to show that many of Gall's teachings were erroneous. By the time Holmes was operating, the detective would surely have been up on the latest scientific papers thoroughly undermining the field. That both Holmes and Moriarty both continued to dabble in it is almost unfathomable, unless we should assume that they did it playfully to shock or to make a point.

Home and Away

Some 60 per cent of the criminals apprehended in the canon came from the United Kingdom, when in reality all but 1.2 per cent of inmates in British prisons during the late Victorian era were homegrown. Of the villains Holmes encountered, almost 20 per cent came from continental Europe and a further 10 per cent from North America. The rest were shared fairly evenly between South America, Australia, Africa and Asia.

A Jewel of a Story

'The Mazarin Stone' is one of only two canonical stories to be narrated in the third-person, the other being 'His Last Bow'. 'The Mazarin Stone' was probably written in this way because it was based on a stage play Conan Doyle had written called *The Crown Diamond*. Although Watson was a featured character in the play, a key element of the dramatic plot involved eavesdropping on a pair of villainous figures – a twist that would have been difficult to render in a first-person narrative. The show debuted on stage in May 1921 (although an early draft was probably written as far back as 1912) and then appeared in its short-story form in *The Strand* in November that year. The narrative underwent a number of changes in that time, most notably Colonel Sebastian Moran being replaced as Holmes's nemesis by Count Negretto Sylvius. The Mazarin stone itself, meanwhile, was named in honour of the famous French power-broker, Cardinal Mazarin. A diplomat with Machiavellian tendencies, Mazarin most famously served as Chief Minister to the French kings, Louis XIII and Louis XIV, during which time he evolved from 'the power behind the throne' to the de facto ruler of the French nation. He would have made a deliciously compelling nemesis for Holmes in another lifetime.

The Play's the Thing

Sherlock Holmes and *The Crown Diamond* were not Conan Doyle's only attempts to transfer his literary son from the page to the stage. In 1910, for example, he wrote and produced a stage version of *The Speckled Band* (originally to have been called *The Stonor Case*). The previous year, Conan Doyle had hired London's Adelphi Theatre to stage a non-Holmes drama called *The House of Temperley*, which was a commercial flop and closed earlier than its playwright had hoped. Under threat of a huge economic loss, Conan Doyle hit upon the idea of unleashing a new Sherlock Holmes play onto the public in the hope of replicating the success Gillette's production had recently enjoyed. The script for *The Stonor Case* was apparently completed in an intense week of writing. A mere two weeks after *The House of Temperley* folded, a company was inside the Adelphi rehearsing the new show. It largely stuck to the plot of the short story on which it was based, with a few names being altered (for instance, the Stoners became the Stonors, Roylott became Rylott, and the dead sister Julia became Violet). H. A. Saintsbury, who had enjoyed huge success in the title role in Gillette's production, reprised the role for Conan Doyle, with Lyn Harding being suitably terrifying as the villain, and Claude King playing Watson. The show opened on 4 June 1910 and ran for 169 performances, before transferring to another West End theatre and then going on a national tour. A New York run followed. Conan Doyle had not only averted financial disaster but had created a fully fledged cash-cow.

THE BOA STAR

The real star of the show in *The Stonor Case* was undoubtedly the snake. While some critics believed they were witnessing a fake beast, Conan Doyle insisted that a very much living rock boa was used, usually turning up for the curtain call draped around the neck of the game Lyn Harding.

Raffle Winner

E. W. Hornung, creator of the Raffles stories, was another writer who took inspiration from Holmes. He was, in addition, Conan Doyle's brother-in-law after marrying Connie Doyle in 1893. Conan Doyle and Hornung even briefly collaborated on a play for Henry Irving the following year before the project was aborted. In 1898, Hornung wrote 'The Ides of March', a short story that introduced the characters of Arthur J. Raffles – gentleman thief and enthusiastic cricketer – and his sidekick and chronicler,

Harry 'Bunny' Manders. It appeared in the June issue of *Cassell's* magazine and featured in a Raffles collection entitled *The Amateur Cracksman* which appeared the following year. In all, Hornung authored twenty-six Raffles short stories, two plays and a novel. The similarities between Raffles and Bunny, on the one hand, and Holmes and Watson, on the other, were obvious even before *The Amateur Cracksman* was dedicated to Conan Doyle. However, he was never quite sure what to make of his brother-in-law's invention. 'I think I may claim that his famous character Raffles was a kind of inversion of Sherlock Holmes, Bunny playing Watson,' he would write.

> He [Hornung] admits as much in his kindly dedication. I think there are few finer examples of short-story writing in our language than these, though I confess I think they are rather dangerous in their suggestion. I told him so before he put pen to paper, and the result has, I fear, borne me out. You must not make the criminal a hero.

Yet in a strange inversion, it seems that Conan Doyle drew at least a little upon the Raffles tales when he was persuaded to bring Holmes back to life in 1903's 'The Empty House'. Critics have drawn parallels between the famous scene in which Holmes reveals his true identity with a similar unmasking scene that featured in Raffles' 'No Sinecure', published in 1901.

Local Rivals

In the 1950s, an opinion poll was conducted to discover the nation's most popular fictional detective. The winner was a now largely forgotten character by the name of Sexton Blake. Sherlock Holmes was not only not the world's favourite investigator, but he was ranked only second among the candidates based in Baker Street – Sexton's own address for a good part of his career. It was a remarkable success for a character who first appeared in 1893 in a very conscious effort to cash in on the success of Conan Doyle's stories. For some eighty-five years, Sexton Blake was the face of an extraordinary franchise that took in short stories and novels, comic strips, radio, TV and the silver screen. He changed with the times, too, migrating from his position as 'the poor man's Sherlock Holmes' to become an international action man.

A CULTURAL PHENOMENON

By the time he was effectively retired in the 1970s, Sexton Blake had featured in around 4,000 stories, authored by some 200 authors and running to several million words. From humble beginnings, Sexton Blake became a cultural phenomenon. Today, though, it is safe to say that Baker Street belongs to only one detective.

Backing the Underdog

Throughout the canon, Holmes is seen gaining as much gratification from proving the innocence of the wrongly accused as from cornering villains. It is a character trait that was also evident in his creator. Conan Doyle repeatedly took up the causes of those he believed had been wronged by the justice system, as he did in the case of George Edalji. But perhaps his most famous attempt to right a wrong concerned the case of Oscar Slater. In December 1908, Marion Gilchrist, a reclusive 83-year-old spinster, was attacked and beaten to death in her Glasgow home. Despite there being several valuable treasures on the premises, the assailant was disturbed and got away with only a brooch. Slater – a petty criminal – lived a few streets away and suspicion fell on him when he was connected to a pawn ticket for a brooch. Moreover, he left the country for New York just a few days later. However, it was a pre-planned trip, the pawn ticket was a red herring and identification evidence was severely compromised. Nonetheless, he was tracked down in America and extradited to face trial for murder. Despite a chronic lack of evidence, he was convicted by majority verdict – amid suspicions that his background (he was a German Jew) had counted against him in the eyes of some. His death sentence was at least commuted to a life sentence in prison and he would go on to serve almost nineteen years. Conan Doyle looked into the case in detail in 1912 and concluded that Slater had been 'framed-up' by a mixture of 'stupidity and dishonesty'. He wrote a book on the case and pressed for a full pardon, which was not forthcoming. In 1914, he again agitated for a judicial review of the verdict but, once more, to no avail. Then, in 1925, a desperate Slater secretly wrote to Conan Doyle from prison to plead for his intervention one more time. Conan Doyle campaigned for his release with renewed vigour and after an arduous two years, Slater was at last granted his freedom. It should have represented an unmitigated triumph – an exhaustive pursuit of justice that rivalled Holmes's own efforts in terms of dogged determination. However, this tale was to have an ultimately unsatisfactory ending. Conan Doyle had spent a small fortune on Slater's behalf, and when Slater was awarded £6,000 in compensation (equivalent to several hundred thousand today), he expected some recompense. For Conan Doyle, it was a matter not of finances but principle. However, Slater, embittered by the hand life had dealt him, had no intention of sharing his windfall. Where Slater had once been the author's *cause célèbre*, he was now seen by Conan Doyle as an ungrateful freeloader.

High Spirits

'This world is big enough for us,' Holmes declared in 'The Sussex Vampire'. 'No ghosts need apply.' As we have already seen in the case of the Cottingley Fairies, the supernatural was an area upon which the opinions of Holmes and Conan Doyle diverged. Generations of Holmes enthusiasts have struggled to reconcile the detective's rejection of other-worldly phenomena with Conan Doyle's wholehearted commitment to spiritualism. In a life marked by extraordinary achievements and passionate campaigning, it was the desire to spread the gospel of spiritualism that came to dominate his life, although his spiritualist beliefs did not come to public notice to any great extent prior to the late 1910s. Some considered it a response to the losses he had suffered in the First World War and its aftermath – he lost both his son, Kingsley, and his brother, Innes, in quick succession, as well as two brothers-in-law (including E.W. Hornung; see page 159) and two nephews. He was certainly not alone in harbouring hopes of being able to reconnect with lost loved ones at that time of industrialized slaughter. In 1918, he published *New Revelation*, an extended essay which was subtitled: *What is Spiritualism?: Can we, or can we not, speak with our beloved dead? Sir Arthur Conan Doyle answers YES*. It marked his arrival as a spiritualist champion and, by the time of his death in 1930, he had authored some twenty titles on the subject – including the landmark *The History of Spiritualism* (1926) – to become perhaps the most famous spiritualist advocate in the world. But Conan Doyle's interest in the subject had actually started much earlier. He began to read widely around the subject in the 1880s and even attended séances while still practising as a doctor. Then in 1893 he joined the British Society for Psychical

Research, a recently established organization devoted to investigating supposedly paranormal phenomena with a scientific vigour. Conan Doyle became satisfied that such phenomena as telepathy had scientific veracity long before he emerged on to the public stage as the poster-boy for spiritualism. He paid a heavy price for his beliefs, however, at once courting controversy and prompting mockery. There was a personal cost, too. The illusionist Harry Houdini, for instance, was a friend who felt the need to break off ties with Conan Doyle after the two fell out over the issue. It is safe to assume Holmes would have sided with Houdini on this particular question.

My Word!

According to word frequency analysis published in the *Guardian* newspaper in 2015, every single canonical case is described as 'singular', 'remarkable' or 'curious'. Moreover, eleven cases are described as both 'singular' and 'remarkable', seven as 'singular' and 'curious', and five as 'remarkable' and 'curious'. Then there are some eighteen cases that are described as 'singular', 'remarkable' and 'curious'!

Value for Money

Despite his phenomenal skills as a detective, Holmes did not profit as much as might be expected. He generally worked on a fixed fee system, and every now and again even offered his services for free. This was, in part, the reason why he came to buddy-up with Watson – so that he might be able to share the strain of an expensive London rent. However, he did manage to enjoy a few significant paydays when the client was sufficiently wealthy. For example, he received £1,000 after recovering the beryl coronet, a further £1,000 for recovering the blue carbuncle, another £1,000 in cash and gold from the King of Bohemia in light of his difficulty with Irene Adler (plus a bonus 'snuffbox of old gold, with a great amethyst in the centre of the lid' for a job well done), and a fine emerald tie-pin from Queen Victoria for his part in protecting national security in the Bruce-Partington affair. It is reasonable to assume he was also well recompensed for his work, which is only alluded to in broad terms, for both the French government and the King of Scandinavia. However, his largest payday that we can be sure about occurred in 'The Priory School' when the Duke of Holdernesse paid him £12,000 for solving a case and being discreet about it.

Love Rat

Holmes was famously unattached in romantic terms. As we have seen, among the women of the canon only Irene Adler in 'A Scandal in Bohemia' seemed to make anything like an enduring impact – earning herself the epithet of 'the woman'. Yet it is often forgotten that Holmes was, albeit briefly, betrothed. In 'Charles Augustus Milverton', he took on the persona of a plumber and ingratiated himself with a housemaid called Agatha. 'You would not call me a marrying man, Watson?', he teased the doctor one day, before adding: 'You'll be interested to hear that I'm engaged.' The motive behind his proposal, he revealed, was a quest for information, with Watson pondering: 'Surely you have gone too far?' It emerged that Holmes had been walking out with the poor dupe each evening, talking extensively with her ('Good heavens, those talks!'). But with her purpose served, he showed her little compassion. In response to Watson's question, 'But the girl, Holmes?', he merely shrugged. 'You can't help it, my dear Watson,' he said. 'You must play your cards as best you can when such a stake is on the table. However, I rejoice to say that I have a hated rival, who will certainly cut me out the instant that my back is turned. What a splendid night it is!' Holmes was many admirable things, but not the sort of chap you'd want your sister to bring home.

The Hounds of Hell

The Hound of the Baskervilles, probably the most famous Sherlock Holmes story of them all, is based on a myth which had already been doing the rounds in Dartmoor – where the novel is set – for over two hundred years when Conan Doyle first heard it. The focal point of the legend was a dastardly local squire who went by the name of Richard Cabell and lived at Brook Hall in the Buckfastleigh district of Devon. He was not much liked by the locals, who were terrorized by his fearsome temper. He was especially known for his love of hunting, his desire to kill defenceless creatures seeming to fit neatly with the general opinion as to his bad nature. However, his blood lust – it was

claimed – did not end with wild animals. He was strongly rumoured to have done away with his unfortunate wife, Elizabeth, the daughter of a baronet.

Cabell was thought to have made a pact with the devil. When he died in 1677, there were few tears shed but he continued to inspire fear even in death. So worried were locals that his wicked spirit would escape the grave that he was buried in a coffin fixed shut with a lid of thick slate, which in turn was enclosed in a specially constructed sepulchre at Holy Trinity Church, Buckfastleigh. But the forces of hell could not be contained, so the legend goes. On the night when his body was interred, a pack of ghoulish spectral hounds raced across the fog-covered moors to howl at his tomb. Ever the hunter, he could be seen for years to come – so said the locals – leading these hell hounds across the moors, especially around the anniversary of his death.

Cabell may well have been a nasty piece of work but today we should perhaps be thankful to him for having sown the seed of an idea that, long after his death, was turned into one of the most enduringly popular sagas in the English language. But be careful if you dare to visit his tomb today . . . they say that if you put your fingers through the bars, the wicked squire will give them a nibble.

Partners in Crime-Writing?

The mystery surrounding the authorship of *The Hound of the Baskervilles* might even have stumped Holmes himself. The question is how much of the story came from the pen of Conan Doyle alone, and how much we owe to his friend, Bertram Fletcher Robinson. Fletcher Robinson was a writer of some note on his own account, not to mention a respected magazine editor. Still only in his early thirties when *The Hound* was published, Fletcher Robinson was responsible for a prodigious output that included some detective stories of his own and collaborations with no lesser figure than P. G. Wodehouse. He had also helmed a number of respected literary journals and would go on to edit *Vanity Fair* magazine. Conan Doyle and Fletcher Robinson had become firm friends when they travelled on the same ship from Cape Town to Southampton in 1900. Early the following year, Fletcher Robinson took his famous friend on a tour of the sights of Dartmoor, an area to which he had moved while he was still a child. It was on this trip that he revealed the legend of Squire Cabell. Conan Doyle and Fletcher Robinson were both blessed with a nose for a good story and the pair agreed to collaborate on a story to be called *The Hound of the Baskervilles*. It was, Conan Doyle wrote to his mother, to be a 'small book' but 'a real creeper'. However, at some point after this Conan Doyle decided to rework the story to make it a Holmes tale. The clamour for more of his detective stories – not to mention the financial incentives to resurrect Holmes – had reached such a level that he could no longer resist. To begin with, Conan Doyle had suggested to his editors that the work should appear under a joint by-line with Fletcher Robinson, but his paymasters were unwilling to dilute the power of the Conan Doyle brand. Instead, the author inserted a footnote into the first chapter: 'This story owes its inception to my friend, Mr Fletcher Robinson, who has helped me both in the general plot and in the local details.' Moreover, he paid Fletcher Robinson £500, a considerable sum in 1901 when the book was first serialized. Bertram Fletcher Robinson never publicly declared that he wrote any of the book himself and Conan Doyle would later declare that 'the plot and every word of the actual narrative are my own'. Yet rumours have persisted that the collaboration went deeper. If not, why suggest a joint by-line and why such a significant payment? In the 1950s, Fletcher Robinson's coachman, Harry Baskerville – whose family name was used in the title of the famous book – suggested Fletcher Robinson had been responsible for large chunks of the book. At the extreme end of things, such rumours have spurred some rather incredible conspiracy theories, including the suggestion that Conan Doyle had a part in his friend's early death. Such talk is generally considered bunkum and most Holmesians remain sceptical that Conan Doyle was anything other than the principle creator of the book – citing, not least, Fletcher Robinson's own silence on the subject – but the question of authorship nonetheless persists, a mystery layered on top of a mystery.

In the Pinkertons

Detectives from the famous American Pinkerton National Detective Agency appear in two of the canonical stories, 'The Red Circle' (1911) and, most famously, in *The Valley of Fear* (1915). The agency was established by Allan Pinkerton, a Scot who emigrated to the States in 1842 and seven years later became a police detective in Chicago. He set up the Pinkertons a year later and came to national prominence when he was said to have foiled an assassination plot against Abraham Lincoln during the US Civil War. In the 1870s, the agency was hired by rich mining interests to disrupt the activities of the so-called Molly Maguires – a secret society with roots in Ireland who riled Pennsylvania mine-owners because of their part in a series of expensive labour disputes. The group was infiltrated by Pinkerton agent James McParland, who arrived in New York from County Armagh in 1867. He became a trusted secretary on one of their branches and fed intelligence back to the authorities, putting himself in considerable personal peril. As a result of the evidence he garnered, some ten members of the organization were hanged. However, their guilt is questioned, amid suspicions that charges were trumped up by a mining industry keen to see the back of them. It was McParland's story in particular that fascinated Conan Doyle as he wrote *The Valley of Fear*. It just so happened that, shortly before publication of that story, the author met William Pinkerton, the son of Allan Pinkerton and by then head of his father's agency. The two seemingly got on well although the friendship was not to last. Pinkerton was unhappy with *The Valley of Fear*, apparently suspecting that Conan Doyle had incorporated elements from their private conversations. Nonetheless, Conan Doyle had likely finished the text before the pair met and had gained his intelligence not from Pinkerton but from another detective, William J. Burns (see next entry). It has been alleged that Pinkerton feared certain details in the story risked exposing family members of McParland to danger. If this was indeed the case, it is safe to assume that Conan Doyle had done so quite unwittingly. It was nonetheless a sad end to a fleeting friendship. For readers of Holmes, there is at least the consolation that the Pinkertons were key elements in such a strong pair of stories before relations soured.

America's Holmes

Being the living embodiment of a fictional legend is burdensome, as Joseph Bell (see page 79) could have told you. A similar fate befell the Irish-American detective, William J. Burns, who Conan Doyle publicly declared was

'America's Sherlock Holmes'. Burns was born in 1861 to parents who had fled Ireland during the potato famine. His interest in the world of criminality was sparked off in his teens when he became friendly with a notorious forger by the name of Charles Ulrich. Opting for the right side of the tracks, Burns got a job with the Columbus Police Department in Ohio, before becoming a private detective, working for Thomas Furlong, whose team offered services similar to those of the Pinkerton Agency. Next, he moved to the Secret Service, and it was there that his reputation burgeoned. He became noted for heading investigations characterized by thorough research, cunning undercover operations and robust interviewing of suspects – all traits that could be seen in Holmes's own practice. Never one to eschew publicity, it was not long before Burns was in a position to set up his own agency. Over the years, his tales of derring-do and his ability to secure arrests made him a quasi-legendary figure. In 1911, for instance, he infiltrated a colony of anarchists in Washington State as he rooted out the notorious McNamara Brothers – responsible for the previous year's bombing of the *Los Angeles Times* building that killed more than twenty and injured a further hundred. On another occasion, Burns exposed the endemic corruption in San Francisco's city hall by going undercover in the city's docks.

The Teapot Dome Scandal

Such were Burns's achievements that in 1921 he was invited to become director of the Bureau of Investigation (forerunner of the modern FBI), but it was here that his fortunes would take a downturn. His reputation suffered badly when Bureau agents investigating the notorious Teapot Dome Scandal (a bribery scandal in which public officials were allegedly paid off by the oil industry) started to threaten journalists critical of President Warren Harding's government. Burns was forced to resign, to be succeeded by none other than J. Edgar Hoover. While Conan Doyle ensured Holmes exited the scene while his public was still hungry to hear more of him, 'the American Sherlock Holmes' alas left his stage under a cloud.

Hands Across the Ocean

Holmes was not much of a political beast, but one of his more explicit political declarations is to be found in the 1892 story, 'The Nobel Bachelor'. Holmes is seen yearning for 'a world-wide country under a flag which shall be a quartering of the Union Jack with the Stars and Stripes'. It is, perhaps, a rather jilting passage that does not quite sound like the detective. There is a good reason for that. Here was an occasion where Holmes was serving as the mouthpiece of Conan Doyle. The Scot was a keen admirer of the American nation, which in turn loved him and Holmes. For evidence, we need look no further than a letter he published in *The Times* on 7 January 1896. In it he spoke of the great kindness he had personally received on a trip to America, along with his concern over a more general anti-English sentiment he had encountered. 'I believe,' he wrote, 'and have long believed, that the greatest danger which can threaten our Empire is the existence of this spirit of hostility in a nation which is already great and powerful, but which is destined to be far more so in the future. Our statesmen have stood too long with their faces towards the East. To discern our best hopes as well as our gravest dangers they must turn them the other way.' The ill-feeling between the two countries had, he recognized, long and deep historical routes, going back to the treatment of the American colonies, but he also cited the unwillingness of the British to recognize the achievements of their American cousins. Where Holmes spoke abstractly of 'a world-wide country' under a joint flag, Conan Doyle now made his pitch for a practical approach. He said:

> Above all, I should like to see an Anglo-American Society started in London, with branches all over the Empire, for the purpose of promoting good feeling, smoothing over friction, laying literature before the public which will show them how strong are the arguments in favour of an Anglo-American alliance, and supplying the English Press with the American side

of the question and vice versa. Such an organization would, I am sure, be easily founded, and would do useful work towards that greatest of all ends, the consolidation of the English-speaking races.

In Holmes, Conan Doyle had gone some way to prove that Britain and the US were not two nations divided by a common language after all.

Family Secrets

In *The Sign of the Four*, it is revealed – albeit obliquely – that Watson suffered a difficult family background that rendered his many achievements and irrepressible enthusiasm all the more remarkable. In that story, we learn that Watson's father had been dead for 'many years', although the cause of his death is never revealed. Moreover, allusion is made to Watson's tragic older brother. Despite the sibling's previous 'good prospects', Holmes deduced from a watch in Watson's possession that he 'threw away his chances, lived for some time in poverty with occasional short intervals of prosperity, and finally, taking to drink, he died'. All of this remained, unsurprisingly, highly sensitive to Watson, who suspected Holmes (erroneously, of course) of making unsolicited enquiries into his background and then passing them off as evidence of his powers of observation. Holmes's behaviour left Watson limping about the room 'with considerable bitterness in my heart', although it is fair to say that his bitterness really sprang from his feelings towards his unhappy family circumstances.

No Casement to Answer

Even though Watson had once deemed Holmes's knowledge of politics to be 'feeble', every now and again the detective emerged as an impassioned patriot. This aspect of his character comes through most starkly in the anti-German tone of the First World War-era in 'His Last Bow'. But it is also detectable in 'The Bruce-Partington Plans' (1912) and even as far back as 'The Naval Treaty' (1893). Conan Doyle was never reticent about expressing his own love of country but, in 1916, he became involved in the disquieting case of Roger Casement, who had been sentenced to death for his attempts to rally German support for an anti-British uprising in Ireland. The Irish-born Casement came to public prominence in the 1890s on account of his work for the British Foreign Office in Africa's Congo Free State. In a shocking report that had international repercussions, he exposed the inhumane treatment of the indigenous people by colonial powers – for example, labourers considered lazy had their hands cut off. It was during his bid to improve the human rights of the local African population that Casement first came into contact with Conan Doyle, and they became firm friends. Casement even accompanied Conan Doyle to a performance of 'The Speckled Band' in 1910 and the Irishman was also the inspiration for the character of Lord John Roxton in the non-Holmesian *The Lost World*. In 1911, Casement joined Conan Doyle as a knight of the realm, so it is easy to imagine the latter's shock when his friend was arrested and charged with high treason. He was accused of having travelled to Germany in the depths of the World War to petition for German support for Irish independence. After making his plea, he was returned to Ireland aboard a German U-boat shortly before the Easter Uprising, an aborted attempt by Irish nationalists in Dublin to wrestle political power from the governing British. Conan Doyle struggled to reconcile the man of virtue he knew with such blatant treachery of the country for which he worked as a public servant. Conan Doyle could put it down to nothing other than that Casement was out of his mind. As he put it in a letter of 1916:

> He was a man of fine character, and that he should in the full possession of his senses act as a traitor to the country which had employed and honoured him is inconceivable to anyone who knew him . . . He was a sick man, however, worn by tropical hardships, and he complained often of pains in his head . . . I have no doubt that he is not in a normal state of mind, and that this unhappy escapade at Berlin is only an evidence of it.

Conan Doyle championed a petition for his release, which counted among its signatories such eminent figures as John Galsworthy, George Bernard Shaw and W. B. Yeats. It did not have the desired impact, though, and Casement was executed on 3 August 1916.

Swings and Roundabouts

Such is the aura that surrounds Holmes that it is easy to forget that several of his canonical adventures ended either in defeat or otherwise unsatisfactorily. In 'The Five Orange Pips', he noted: 'I have been beaten four times – three times by men, and once by a woman.' In fact, the argument can be made that over the course of his career – in which his win-rate was undeniably remarkable – there were several more reversals than this quotation indicates. The identity of the woman is most certainly Irene Adler, whose powers of observation, quick-wittedness and spirit so captivated the detective in 'A Scandal in Bohemia'. But the identities of the male rivals who bested him is less clear. The antagonists in 'The Engineer's Thumb' managed to evade justice, so their leader might be considered to have won a victory over Holmes. Similarly, the villains in 'The Five Orange Pips' were never officially caught, although arguably the natural elements had a part to play in their 'escape'. Then there is the criminal at work in 'The Red-Headed League' – I am being deliberately vague as to character names to avoid spoilers as much as possible – who Holmes considers 'the fourth smartest man in London, and for daring I am not sure that he has not a claim to be third'. The detective admits to having previously had 'one or two little turns' with this fellow who 'is at the head of his profession'. That he was still working his nefarious schemes in 'The Red-Headed League' suggests Holmes had not been especially successful against him in these earlier encounters. And then there is Professor Moriarty, that Napoleon of Crime, who Holmes desired so much to deliver into the hands of the courts, but who for so long dodged detection. Surely he must have been one of the four to whom Holmes referred? As for other 'failures' in the Holmes record, he did manage to lose a client in 'The Dancing Men', although whether it was really in his gift to have saved the poor unfortunate is debatable. 'The Yellow Face', meanwhile, is a curiosity in that Holmes spends most of the story barking entirely up the wrong tree.

Norbury

'The Adventure of the Yellow Face' was set in the area of London called Norbury and Holmes so recognized his shortcomings in the investigation that he told Watson to whisper 'Norbury' in his ear should he ever be getting too big for his boots. Muhammad Ali is widely considered the greatest boxer of all time for his brilliance that shone through despite the odd defeat, and Holmes is similarly permitted the occasional failure. Indeed, it is in defeat that he is perhaps at his most humane, while the setbacks bring into sharp relief his extraordinary record of success.

Life, the Universe and Everything

In *A Study in Scarlet*, Watson came across a marked-up article, ambitiously entitled 'The Book of Life'. It 'attempted to show how much an observant man might learn by an accurate and systematic examination of all that came in his way' and was, in Watson's immediate judgement, 'ineffable twaddle!'

'From a drop of water,' said the writer, 'a logician could infer the possibility of an Atlantic or a Niagara without having seen or heard of one or the other. So all life is a great chain, the nature of which is known whenever we are shown a single link of it . . . The Science of Deduction and Analysis,' insisted the writer, 'is one which can only be acquired by long and patient study nor is life long enough to allow any mortal to attain the highest possible perfection in it.' The writer was, of course, Holmes himself. Facing Watson's scepticism, he explained that he had 'a turn both for observation and for deduction'. It is partly as a result of this exchange that Holmes is regarded as the master of deduction – the skill of moving from an accepted premise to a specific conclusion. An example of deduction might be to say that all apples are fruit, so all Braeburns must be fruits, too. However, this is only a single strand of Holmes's method of detection. More often, we see him practising inductive reasoning – extrapolating conclusions about unobserved events from observed evidence. A man lies dead. A bloody knife lies beside him. He was probably stabbed. The more information gathered, the more secure the conclusion becomes, hence Holmes's assertion: 'When you have eliminated all which is impossible, then whatever remains, however improbable, must be the truth.' But Holmes also employed a related technique – that of abductive reasoning, where observed evidence is used to find the most likely explanation for the existence of that evidence, without being able to categorically prove the thesis. A post-mortem examination will reveal if our victim died from stab wounds. A letter lies on the floor nearby, to the victim from his wife. She has fallen in love with another and has fled abroad to start a new life. Did reading the letter prompt the victim to take his own life? We cannot be sure but the evidence would suggest a strong probability. So, the Master of Deduction should really be considered the Master of Abduction.

Scouting for Heroes

Like much of the British population of his age, Conan Doyle was an admirer of Robert Baden-Powell, who had achieved national hero status when he led a force of a few hundred soldiers and civilians against a besieging force of several thousand Boers in the South African town of Mafeking. He held off the Boers for a total of 217 days before relieving British forces arrived, in what was regarded as an outstanding example of military leadership. The siege ran from the end of 1899 into early 1900, just as the Second Boer War was getting into full swing. In 1900, Conan Doyle wrote his rallying call to the British people, *The Great Boer War*, in which he described Baden-Powell in these terms:

> Colonel Baden-Powell is a soldier of a type which is exceedingly popular with the British public. A skilled hunter and an expert at many games, there was always something of the sportsman in his keen appreciation of war . . . There was a brain quality in his bravery which is rare among our officers. Full of veldt craft and resource, it was as difficult to outwit as it was to outfight him. But there was another curious side to his complex nature . . . An impish humour broke out in him, and the mischievous schoolboy alternated with the warrior and the administrator.

It should thus perhaps come as little surprise that Holmes – with whom he seemed to share a number of traits – appealed to Baden-Powell. In his military manual, *Aids to Scouting for N.C.O.s and Men*, written just a few months before the siege of Mafeking, he named the Sherlock Holmes stories as recommended reading for all cavalry Scouts. He wanted them to pick up tips on tracking and deductive reasoning from the master. He adapted much of that text for his book *Scouting for Boys*, which helped launch the modern Scouting movement in 1908. Again, Holmes featured prominently, with the text making no less than six references to the detective or his real-life counterpart, Joseph Bell. He also suggested to Scout leaders that they hone their boys' deductive skills by setting up 'crimes' for the Scouts to solve, either using the canonical tales as a blueprint or else devising cases of their own. In his 1933 biography, *Lessons from the Varsity of Life*, Baden-Powell again emphasized the importance of the Holmes example to the military man:

When I went scouting with Fred Burnham [who taught Baden-Powell woodcrafting in Rhodesia], he was quicker than I in noticing 'sign', but in pointing it out to me he would ask: 'Here, Sherlock, what do you make of this?' Unfortunately we British make very little use of the art, either in our military or civil training, so when we go on service, not being accustomed to tracking habitually, we often neglect to use it, even when the ground before us lies open like a book, full of information . . . There was a lot of Sherlock Holmes work to be done in our job.

His Master's Voice

Of the sixty canonical stories, Holmes narrates just two himself. These were 'The Lion's Mane' and 'The Blanched Soldier', both late stories dating to 1926. 'The Lion's Mane', notable for exposing one of the most unexpected killers in the canon, had good reason not to be narrated by Watson. It is set during Holmes's retirement and the good doctor was simply not there. 'The Blanched Soldier' is different, though. It is set in 1903 and begins with a justification for the choice of narrator.

> The ideas of my friend Watson, though limited, are exceedingly pertinacious. For a long time he has worried me to write an experience of my own. Perhaps I have rather invited this persecution, since I have often had occasion to point out to him how superficial are his own accounts and to accuse him of pandering to popular taste instead of confining himself rigidly to facts and figures. 'Try it yourself, Holmes!' he has retorted, and I am compelled to admit that, having taken my pen

in my hand, I do begin to realize that the matter must be presented in such a way as may interest the reader.

It is a brave admission on the part of Holmes, but also, by proxy, on the part of Conan Doyle. The absence of the mediating presence of Watson is felt in all those stories that he does not tell. For many readers, the Holmes-told or third-person narrations do not quite come up to scratch. Holmes himself arguably nailed the problem in 'The Blanched Soldier'. Watson is, he said, 'one to whom each development comes as a perpetual surprise, and to whom the future is always a closed book'. In other words, he stands in for the reader on adventures, knowing as little as we do about what is coming next. It is his wide-eyed wonder at what might lay ahead that gives the stories their energy and perhaps explains why Holmes was allowed to wield the pen himself only twice.

The Bee-All and End-All

We learn from the canon that Holmes retired (in truth, semi-retired) from the world of detection in 1903, moving to the rolling hills of the Sussex Downs, a few miles from Eastbourne on the English south coast. There, despite increasing problems with rheumatism, Holmes became an apiarist – that is to say, a bee-keeper. This being Holmes, however, he was not content to dabble in his new hobby

but looked instead to utterly master it. The result was a tome going under the title of *The Practical Handbook of Bee Culture, With Some Observations Upon the Segregation of the Queen.* In certain respects, this change of lifestyle might be considered emblematic of Holmes returning to his roots in old age. He was, after all, descended from a line of country squires. But in apiary he also found a pastime that allowed him to practise many of the same skills that he had wielded so effectively as a detective. For him, a bee colony represented a complete society to be observed and understood, a world to be intellectually conquered.

His handbook, then, was not so much a retreat into rural tranquillity but was instead 'the fruit of pensive nights and laborious days when I watched the little working gangs as once I watched the criminal world of London'.

And so, the man whose intellectual brilliance had struck fear into the hearts of the nation's criminals ended his days, fittingly, as the master of all he surveyed.

SELECTED BIBLIOGRAPHY

Conan Doyle, A., *Memories and Adventures* (Hodder & Stoughton, 1924)

Conan Doyle, A., *The Penguin Complete Sherlock Holmes* (Penguin, 1981)

Haining, P. (ed.), *A Sherlock Holmes Companion* (Barnes & Noble, 1980)

Haining, P. (ed.), *The Sherlock Holmes Scrapbook* (Reed Editions, 1987)

Lellenberg, J., Stashower, D. and Foley, C. (eds), *Arthur Conan Doyle – A Life in Letters* (HarperPress, 2007)

Lycett, A., *Conan Doyle – The Man Who Created Sherlock Holmes* (Weidenfeld & Nicolson, 2007)

Nown, G., *Elementary, My Dear Watson: Sherlock Holmes Centenary – His Life and Times* (Ward Lock, 1986)

O'Brien, J., *The Scientific Sherlock Holmes: Cracking the Case with Science and Forensics* (OUP, 2013)

The Sherlock Holmes Journal (the Sherlock Holmes Society of London, 1952–)

Smith, D., *The Ardlamont Mystery: The Real-Life Story Behind the Creation of Sherlock Holmes* (Michael O'Mara Books, 2018)

Tracey, J., *The Encyclopaedia Sherlockiana* (Jack Doubleday & Co., 1977)

Wagner, E. J., *The Science of Sherlock Holmes: From Baskerville Hall to the Valley of Fear, the Real Forensics Behind the Great Detective's Greatest Cases* (John Wiley & Sons, 2007)